MODERN LITURGY Answers

the 101 Most-Asked Questions about Liturgy

Nick Wagner

Resource Publications, Inc.
San Jose, California

Editorial director: Nick Wagner
Prepress manager: Elizabeth J. Asborno

Reprint Department
Resource Publications, Inc.
160 E. Virginia Street #290
San Jose, California 95112-5876
(408) 286-8505

Library of Congress Cataloging in Publication Data
Wagner, Nick, 1957-
    Modern Liturgy answers the 101 most-asked questions about liturgy / Nick Wagner.
        p.   cm.
    Includes bibliographical references and index.
    ISBN 0-89390-369-8
    1. Catholic Church—Liturgy—Miscellanea. I. Title.
    BX1970.W255   1996
    264'.02—dc20   96-3639

Printed in the United States of America

00 99 98 97 96 | 5 4 3 2 1

Contents

Ministers

Art & Environment

Seasons

Sacraments

Preface

Anyone who cares about liturgy would do well to know how to bake bread. Bread, and all that goes into it, bears the mystery of our faith.

Bread begins as the seed that falls to the earth and dies. From that death, the seed grows new wheat. The wheat, once harvested, is separated from the chaff. Farmers give their lives to grow the wheat, suffering through the caprices of weather and soil conditions, eventually delivering the wheat to the mills. Millers grind the wheat, converting it into something new. The wheat-made-new, the pure flour, is given over to the baker. The baker mixes the flour, combining it with water and again transforming the "wheat" into something new. This new thing, the dough, is kneaded, shaped, cut, punched, and finally baked in the ovens.

The wheat is transformed by the fire and heat of the ovens to become food for the flock. Just as the Christ-child was laid in the manger to become food for the flock, this fired wheat is offered at our altars to become the Christ-food for us. The bread of life is broken, as Christ is broken on the cross. The broken Christ-bread becomes one again when we take his Body into our individual bodies. We are all mixed together, as flour and water are mixed, to make something new. The broken bread becomes a whole body, *the* Body, made new for the sake of the world.

All the rest is prelude and epilogue. To bake bread is to be the paschal mystery of Christ's passion, death, and resurrection.

This is a kind of recipe book to help make better bakers. Some steps you may already know. Others may be things you once knew and have forgotten. And still others may be new to you and give you new flavorings to put in your liturgical bread.

May the Body of Christ bring us all to everlasting life.

Nick Wagner
Advent 1995

Groundwork
Questions

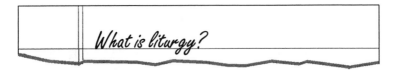

What is liturgy?

"Liturgy" comes from the Greek word *leitourgia*. It literally means "the people's work." In the ancient Greek cultures, it originally meant civic duty or the cooperation of all citizens to make society work.

The religious meaning is similar. Liturgy is the work that all Christians do to make our tradition, our beliefs, our faith, work in our lives and in the world. It is in the liturgy where we are most truly church. It is in the liturgy where we become the Body of Christ.

Liturgy is not synonymous with Mass. Mass is one kind of liturgy. There are many other kinds as well. All liturgies have three things in common:

1. they are rituals

2. they are prayers

3. they are communal

"Communal" is a key word here. Catholics have some prayer rituals that are not "communal." These non-liturgical prayers are often called devotions and are a very important part of our faith lives. But all devotions derive from and lead to liturgical prayer. When we say liturgy is communal, we mean that the ritual prayer in question is one in which the church as a whole has always found and celebrated the core elements of our faith. Some examples of liturgies include the Mass, Liturgy of the Word, Liturgy of the Hours, all the sacraments, and ritual blessings such as those found in the *Book of Blessings*.

Liturgies are also prayers. Prayer, in the sense used here, does not mean becoming quiet and talking to God. Instead it means listening to and being obedient to God. Sometimes we need to be quiet to listen to God. But more often, especially in the liturgy, "listening" has more to do with paying attention than being quiet. In the liturgy, we proclaim, sing, move, share, bless, etc. All these actions are ways of being in the world. By doing these things in a particular way, they carry particular meaning. Those meanings communicate to us and to others our beliefs. By fully participating

3

in these actions, we more fully understand their meanings and more deeply immerse ourselves in faith. It is in this way we "listen" to God. It is in this way we pray.

The way we do these actions is set down in a pattern. The pattern of behavior is a ritual. Liturgy is ritual. Some people think ritual stifles their creativity and their individuality. Christians, especially Catholic Christians, do not believe that. By practicing a set, patterned behavior, we become so familiar with the ritual that we can use it as a foundation for growth. Musicians know this. Musicians cannot fully express themselves in their music until they have mastered the techniques of the instrument. They repeat pattern after pattern, day after day, year after year, to get to a place where they can express what they want to with their music. And yet they never reach perfection.

Christians are the same way. Before we can really "say" what we believe, we have to master the basics of our belief. We do that in ritual prayer.

How does ritual work?

Ritual is a system of symbols that gives meaning to our lives. When we say "Good morning" to someone or "How are you?" we are engaging in ritual. We do not really know the full extent of what people mean when they say these things. But the meaning goes far beyond the literal meaning of the sentences. The meaning has to do with living in and building a civilized society.

If you hear "Good morning" from people you know are not "morning people," for instance, you know they do not literally mean the morning is good. They hate mornings. They mean something like, "Society expects that I acknowledge other human beings in my immediate vicinity, and I want to be a good member of society. Even though I'm feeling pretty antisocial right now, I believe civilization is a good thing. Now that I've done my share to contribute to its upbuilding, I'd appreciate it if you would hand me that cup of coffee and leave me alone until noon."

It is clear from this that ritual has nothing to do with the way a person feels. We sometimes say ritual is empty when it does not reflect our actual feelings. That is not true. Ritual often fails to reflect feelings. The joyful liturgies of Christmas or the penitential mood of Lent may not reflect how we feel on a given Sunday. But it is important that the ritual carry on even though we may not have an internal feeling that reflects the external prayer. That is because ritual reflects and instills values. Ritual is only empty when it no longer instills values the society believes in.

In the above example, the phrase "Good morning" is symbolic. It symbolizes the speaker's unsaid feelings about society and more. As a symbol, the phrase points to a reality that is much greater than the fact that the morning is good. The speaker is symbolically saying he or she believes in that greater reality and, in saying so, helps create that greater reality.

Ritual takes many such symbols and puts them in a pattern in such a way that they tell a story about what the society using the ritual believes.

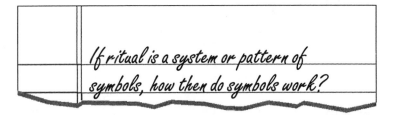

If ritual is a system or pattern of symbols, how then do symbols work?

Symbols are objects, behaviors, or words that help us grasp realities that would otherwise be unknowable. If you want to drive a stake through a liturgist's heart (symbolically, of course) point to one of the major elements of the liturgy and say, "It's *just* a symbol."

That phrase, which many of us say often, implies the object in question lacks a fullness and is not quite real. Symbols, in the sense we are speaking of them here, are the only reality we know. Or, at least, they are the only medium we have for communicating the reality we know. The words on this page, the letters, the sentences, the fact that they are in a pattern we recognize as the English language, the fact that they are in a book that we read from left to right, top to bottom, are all symbols that communicate meaning. We could say the *meaning* of the words is what is important and not the words themselves. But the meaning of a word and the word itself are integrally linked.

The symbols of the liturgy function the same way. Fire means one thing, water another, bread another, and song another. All these symbols somehow help us grasp the reality of God, who would otherwise be unknowable. But each of these symbols says something different about God. They help us understand God from different angles and different levels.

Another important thing about symbols is they have multiple meanings. If you take a moment to free-associate everything you know about water, you will find dozens if not hundreds of meanings. Some of these meanings will be contradictory. For example, water can mean life or it can mean death, depending upon the circumstances.

What water tells us about God is that God can mean life or God can mean death. That is the essence of the paschal mystery—Christ died and rose.

When the many symbols of our faith are organized into ritual patterns, they tell the story of our faith. The pattern itself becomes a symbol. So in the Mass, Word and Eucharist is a symbolic structure. God calls us to faith (Word), and we respond in faith (Eucharist).

Since symbols are the way in which we communicate the reality of our faith, it is important that our symbols be of high quality and be full and rich. When we use water, for example, in order for the water to communicate both life and death, we have to use much more than a spoonful. We need enough water so we can be plunged into it, enough so it speaks as powerfully as possible the reality we want to communicate.

What is the paschal mystery?

The paschal mystery is simple to define but takes a lifetime to understand. It is the mystery of Christ's passion, death, and resurrection. More than that, however, it is the mystery of how God has joined us to that saving mystery so that we, as church, *are* Christ, dead and risen.

The word "paschal" comes from the Greek word *pascha*, which in turn comes from the Hebrew *pesach*. The *pesach* is the Passover celebration by which the Jewish people commemorate the angel of death "passing over" their homes in Egypt and their own "passing over" the Red Sea out of the slavery of Egypt and into the promised land.

St. Paul and the other early church leaders associated Jesus with the Passover lamb which was sacrificed for the sake of the community. Through death, Christ "passed over" from the slavery of this world into the freedom of God's glory. With his death, Christ put to death all the sin and evil of the world. By our baptism, we are joined to that death—and the freedom from slavery to sin that it brings. This is the core of our belief.

It is this core belief—the paschal mystery—that we celebrate every Sunday in the Eucharist. By celebrating it, we enter more fully into the saving death of Christ. We die more completely to ourselves. We become less and less, and Christ becomes more and more.

In addition, each time we celebrate this mystery, our celebration ends in a dismissal. We are dismissed not merely to disperse but to go out into the world and live the mystery we have just celebrated. By joining to Christ in death, we learn to sacrifice ourselves for the sake of the community. We become authentic witnesses to Christ by doing works of justice and living lives of peace. By being transformed in our baptism and in our weekly Eucharist, we in turn, through Christ, transform the world.

This is the faith we proclaim every time we sing, "Christ has died, Christ is risen, Christ will come again." It is the mission we commit to when we are offered the body and blood of Christ in communion, and we pledge, "Amen."

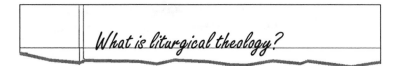

What is liturgical theology?

Theology is the study of God. Theologians try to understand who God is through a philosophical science. But most theology is secondary. That is, we all have an experience of God. We do not need philosophical sciences to tell us we have had that experience. Theology is a systematic reflection on the experience we have already had. The experience is first. The theology is second.

But it is different with liturgy. As individuals, we come to know and experience God in many different ways. But as a church, as a public body of believers, we experience the fullness of God, the "real presence" of God, primarily in the celebration of the liturgy.

This being the case, we say liturgy is primary theology. Another way the church has expressed this idea is by saying, "As the church prays, so it believes." In other words, if you want to know first and foremost what Christians believe about God, look at the way they pray ritually as a community.

You can do this in two ways. You can go to lots of worship services and observe the way Christians pray. This is, in fact, what most people do who want to know what we believe. But suppose you wanted to make a fuller examination of Christian belief. Then, besides experiencing actual worship events, you could study the liturgical prayer books or ritual books of the community. Most Catholics do not realize what a wonderful catechetical resource these books are. The Mass has a prayer book or ritual book called a missal and every sacrament has a ritual book as well. Each of these books has an introduction, which gives directions and explanations about the ritual. Also, the ritual itself contains instructions within it, giving directions about posture, gestures, minister's parts, vessels, symbols, and more. And the prayers themselves tell us something about the public belief of the community. All these ritual books are available somewhere in your parish—usually in the sacristy. They are also available in study editions from Catholic book stores.

What is liturgical catechesis?

Liturgical catechesis is sometimes thought to be a new trend in the church; however, it dates from the New Testament era. The first example we have of liturgical catechesis is the Emmaus story (Lk 24:13-35). In that story, two friends were on a journey to the town of Emmaus. They had been followers of Jesus but were now uncertain of their commitment because Jesus had died. Yet they had heard an extraordinary bit of news. Apparently, Jesus had recently been seen alive by some other followers.

As they were discussing these things, they were joined by a third person, who reminded them of many things Jesus had said. He stirred their faith and their interest. They invited the stranger to walk with them and eventually share dinner with them. Then, as the stranger broke the bread for the meal, they recognized him as Jesus.

This "breaking of the bread" was the same breaking of the bread Jesus had done at the Last Supper. It was the same breaking of the bread that was done in the very early liturgy of the New Testament era. For those followers, that ritual provided insight and clarity about who Jesus was, which is the crux of catechesis. The goal of catechesis is to know Jesus. It is in the liturgy—the breaking of the bread—that we most clearly see who Jesus is and come to know him.

"*Liturgical* catechesis," then, is almost a redundancy. All catechesis is ultimately liturgical in that all catechesis leads to and flows from the liturgy. It is important, however, to distinguish between *catechesis* and *religious education*. Catechesis is necessarily educational, but education is only a means to an end. Education without faith is not catechesis. It is possible, for example, to learn quite a bit about the history, doctrine, and rituals of Catholicism without having any faith in Jesus. It is also possible to learn a very minimal amount about history, doctrine, and rituals and yet have great faith. While catechesis can and does happen in a religious education program and a catechetical process does involve education, faith is the first goal of catechesis.

Liturgical catechesis is structured around the lectionary, the shape of the liturgy, and the rhythm of the church year. By celebrating our faith through these sacred symbols and by reflecting on them in small faith-sharing groups, we come to learn all the essential elements of the faith. There is yet to be written a catechism that is more comprehensive and more nurturing to the faith than the liturgy itself.

What is the liturgical movement?

The liturgical movement began in the 1800s when a Frenchman named Prosper Guéranger refounded the Benedictine Abbey of

Solesmes. In an attempt to revitalize a nation dispirited by the excesses of the Enlightenment, Guéranger believed he could reestablish the liturgical values of the pre-Enlightenment era and thereby revive a faithful hope in Christ. Guéranger's and his brother monks' interest in the liturgy spurred a revival across the whole church, and the Benedictines, remaining true to their traditional concern for the liturgy, were at the forefront of the revival.

At the beginning of this century, the liturgical movement got underway in earnest when Pope Pius X issued a document on sacred music in 1910. Pius X provided the cornerstone for what would become the main thrust of the movement and, eventually, the cornerstone of the liturgical reform called for by the Second Vatican Council. He believed that more active participation by the faithful was essential for developing a true Christian spirit.

A few years later, in 1914, the man who has come to be seen as the founder of the modern liturgical movement, Dom Lambert Beauduin, published his book *La Piété de l'Église*. By developing an understanding of the true meaning of the Body of Christ and how we all participate in and become part of that body in the liturgy, Beauduin made the link between liturgy and social justice that was integral to making the liturgy an action connected with the everyday lives of the people who celebrate it. In the late 1920s the liturgical movement came to the United States due to the tireless efforts of Dom Virgil Michel, a monk at St. John's Abbey in Collegeville, Minnesota. Michel studied in Europe and sponged up every drop of information that he could locate about the liturgical movement. Back at St. John's he began a three-pronged effort to implement the goals of the movement: reform the liturgy, which he helped accomplish by founding *Worship* magazine (originally *Orate Fratres*); reform liturgical and religious education, which he helped accomplish by founding the Liturgical Press, through which he published popular leaflets, catechisms, and translations of the European liturgical scholars; and reform the social structures to be more just, which he was beginning to make headway with when he died unexpectedly at age forty-seven.

The movement grew in both the academic arena and in a grassroots fashion in both the United States and Europe. However, after Pius X, Rome remained silent about all the activity. It was not until 1947 that Pius XII issued the next important liturgical document, the encyclical *Mediator Dei*. It is hard for those of us who have experienced the radical reform of the Second Vatican Council to fully understand how astounding *Mediator Dei* was in its time. For those who could not see the coming council on the still-too-distant horizon, *Mediator Dei* was the *Magna Carta* of the liturgical movement. In this letter, the first papal encyclical dedicated entirely to the subject of the liturgy, the pope called for the participation of the laity in the liturgy with full understanding. Some read between the lines here, seeing this statement as a step toward vernacular liturgy in the future. The direct result of this document was the restoration of the Easter Vigil in 1951 and the reform of all of Holy Week in 1955. Now, for the first time in centuries, the annual celebration of the paschal mystery was again at the center and high point of the church year and the liturgical life of the faithful.

However, it was the Second Vatican Council that manifested the full effect of the liturgical movement. The reform of the liturgy was the first topic taken up by the council, and the growing pressure for liturgical reform was in no small part responsible for John XXIII calling the council in the first place.

With the promulgation of the *Constitution on the Sacred Liturgy* on December 4, 1963, which was approved by the bishops by a vote of 2,147 to 4, the primary goal of the liturgical movement became the will of the universal church. (The date was exactly four centuries from the day, December 4, 1563, that the Council of Trent turned over to the pope the job of reforming the liturgy of that time.) The goal of the liturgical movement—and now of the entire church—was the worship of God through the "full, conscious, and active participation of the laity" in the liturgy and in the life of the church. The most dramatic change that was to enhance that participation was the permission given to celebrate the liturgy in the vernacular.

The 1960s and 1970s, especially in the United States, were times of great excitement and experimentation in the liturgy. The guitar Mass was born, lay people began to serve in liturgical ministries formerly reserved to the ordained, people learned to receive communion in their hands while standing instead of kneeling, and church architecture began to take on new shapes to accommodate the new liturgy.

In the 1980s, Pope John Paul II began to comment on possible excesses of the reform. He sought to slow immoderate liturgical experimentation. Still, John Paul II was one of the bishops at the Second Vatican Council and has always been a strong supporter of the reforms brought about by the council.

11

The liturgical movement of the '90s is quieter, more theological, more focused on smoothing some of the rough edges left by the hurried efforts of the earlier decades. The liturgical pioneers of the pre-Vatican II era number fewer each year, and it seems there are none of similar stature to take their places. There are many fewer priests than in past years, and the clergy have borne much of the work of making the reform a pastoral reality.

Now that fewer priests are available, there are more theologically trained lay people in the church than ever before. And an amazing number of lay volunteers have spent countless hours, usually at their own expense, in adult education. Dioceses, through workshops and certification courses, are still working to carry out the vision of the early reformers.

And the new generation of potential leaders, now in their twenties and thirties, have little or no memory of the pre-Vatican II church. That has advantages and disadvantages. One thing is for sure, however. When they begin to take on leadership roles, their vision of what the church can become will be much more than we might be able to imagine.

The liturgical movement still has not met all its goals. Chief among them is the connection between liturgy and justice. A more active liturgical participation on our part ought, according to Pius X, generate a true Christian spirit. And yet the world is in many ways less spiritual since the Second Vatican Council.

Another important goal that has not been fully met is the full inculturation of the liturgy in the various countries and ethnic populations of the world. It will be up to the leaders of the next decades to find ways to fully implement the reform mandated by the Second Vatican Council.

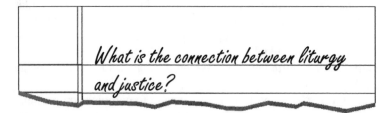

What is the connection between liturgy and justice?

The liturgy is a microcosm. In the liturgy we tell a story. In telling the story, we create a little world. In that little world, inside the walls of the church, gathered around the Lord's Table, we create a world of relationships. These relationships are based on the values of the Gospel.

To say that the relationships in our microcosm, our little world, are based on the values of the Gospel is to say we treat one another as Christ treats us. In that hour of the Mass, we *become* Christ for one another and to one another.

But our relationships with our friends are not the only relationships in our little world. On any given Sunday there is some stranger among us. There is a person we do not know or maybe a person we know but have avoided. There is somebody we consider to be "different" or "other" than us. Yet we are bound by the story we tell, the story of the Gospel, to welcome that person to the table along with everyone else. Even though that person is a stranger, he or she gets treated like one of us.

There is still another relationship. The unknown stranger is not the only person at Mass who is "different" from us. God is also present. Fundamentally, God is a stranger to us. God is "different." God is "other." God can know us, but we cannot know God. Or rather, we cannot know God to such a degree that God ever stops being total mystery to us. Yet it is this God—who is different and strange and other—who invites us to the banquet table. And, because of the story we tell, we accept the invitation.

The purpose of the liturgy, however, is not just microcosmic, not just concerned with our little world. In the liturgy, everyone, friend or stranger, is treated as we would treat our own. Everyone is treated not only justly but lovingly and respectfully. The actions we do and the story we tell are meant to shape our hearts so that we will go out from the liturgy and redo in the world what we have just done in the Mass. That is, we are to go out and not just be fair to people but go so far as to be caring and respectful to strangers. We are to welcome even people who are so different from us that we might consider them "enemies."

If we really understand what we do at liturgy, it has to change the way we live in the world. If everyone who participates regularly in liturgy lived in the world as though the liturgy made a difference in their lives, the world would be a more just, more hospitable place. The challenge to the pastoral leader is to make the liturgy so effective as a story that the celebrators cannot help but be drawn in and changed. The challenge to the individual is to celebrate the liturgy as though it mattered and then to go and put into practice what was just celebrated.

Liturgical
Documents

What is a missal?

The missal is the book the presider uses for the prayers of the Mass. It is usually red, although there is no rule about its color. Originally the missal included the sacramentary, the lectionary, a song book or *antiphonary*, and a list of the order of Masses and readings or *ordo*. As private Masses became more common and the participation of the laity in the liturgy became less common, it became convenient to have all these books combined for the priest. The ultimate form of the missal was the *Missale Romanum* compiled by the Council of Trent in the sixteenth century. Due to the invention of the printing press, this missal could be mass produced and sent to every corner of the world. It was the first time Mass became uniformly standardized.

The missal underwent minor revisions from time to time but remained mostly unchanged until the Second Vatican Council. At that time, the books of the Mass were again separated, the two most significant being the sacramentary and the lectionary.

The current Latin version of the missal contains four parts. It begins with an "Apostolic Constitution" or statement from Pope Paul VI declaring the new missal to be the official order of Mass for the church. Next comes an introduction that is a lengthy justification of the new missal. This was not part of the original document. It was added after several attackers claimed the missal was not orthodox. The introduction is a kind of "catechism" on the missal. It explains the history of the Roman Missal from Trent to Vatican II, the faithfulness of both the Tridentine and the Vatican II missals to the teaching of the church, and the norms followed in the reform. The third part is the *General Instruction of the Roman Missal*, which is more fully described in a following question. The final part is the actual sacramentary itself. (The U.S. version also contains a foreword and appendix to the *General Instruction for the Dioceses of the United States*, the *Directory for Masses with Children*, and the *General Norms for the Liturgical Year and the Calendar*.)

These documents are collected in a book referred to as the sacramentary, but it also retains the title "Roman Missal." The sacramentary—or more correctly, the Mass—underwent significant revision at the Second Vatican Council.

The primary revisions were to streamline the Mass, making the structure of Word and Eucharist more apparent, and to translate the Mass into the vernacular.

The English-language sacramentary is currently undergoing another revision. This is a comparatively minor revision. It consists of retranslating the original Latin into more poetic and more contemporary English, composing some new prayers in English, and making minor adjustments to some of the ritual guidelines for the Mass. Some other countries have already completed a similar revision of their sacramentaries.

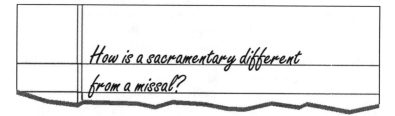

How is a sacramentary different from a missal?

Traditionally, a missal included all the books used for the Mass—the sacramentary, the lectionary, the antiphonary, and the ordo. The sacramentary is a book of prayers the presider needs for the Mass. Scholars are not clear about exactly how the sacramentary came into being. There was no sacramentary, of course, in the early church. The leaders of the Eucharist would pray as they knew best, often drawing on their Jewish heritage of prayer forms. Even the eucharistic prayer was a spontaneous prayer, although it followed a set pattern. In the third and fourth centuries, as the church moved further and further from its Jewish roots and presiders grew less and less skilled at spontaneous prayer, some of the prayers of the Mass began to be set down in small collections know as *libelli*. These were probably not actually used in the Mass but were more likely reference texts for presiders. True sacramentaries began to be assembled in the seventh or eighth century. By the tenth and eleventh centuries, sacramentaries were being copied and multiplied in great number. By the twelfth and thirteenth centuries, almost every parish church had a sacramentary. However, it would have been difficult to find any two that matched exactly. These sacramentaries contained prayers and rubrics for Mass that came from all over Christendom.

What is a lectionary?

A lectionary is a collection of readings from the Bible, which are set down in a particular order to be read at Mass or other liturgies.

Our current lectionary comes from a mandate of the Second Vatican Council stating that "the treasures of the Bible...be opened up more lavishly, so that richer fare may be provided for the faithful at the table of God's Word. In this way a more representative portion of the holy Scriptures will be read to the people over a set cycle of years" (*Constitution on the Sacred Liturgy* 51).

The revision of the lectionary after the Second Vatican Council is one of the major successes of the reform. The current lectionary is not so much a revision as it is a brand new creation. Never in the history of the church was such a comprehensive study done on the lectionary.

The Sunday lectionary is divided into three cycles that correspond to the first three Gospels—Year A for Matthew, Year B for Mark, and Year C for Luke. The Gospels are read in a semi-continuous fashion over the Sundays of the year. A new cycle begins every year on the first Sunday of Advent.

The first reading relates to or foreshadows the Gospel reading. A psalm serves as a response to the first reading. Finally, the second reading is a selection from one of the New Testament letters or from the Acts of the Apostles. These are also read in a semi-continuous fashion and, as a result, often do not correspond to the Gospel reading. The great feasts will sometimes deviate from this general pattern.

The Gospel of John is used extensively in Year B, the year of Mark, because Mark is the shortest Gospel. It is also read during the scrutinies on the third, fourth, and fifth Sundays of Lent every year; the Passion from John's Gospel is read every Good Friday. The Gospel of John did not receive its own year because its outline is very different from the other three Gospels, and it would have been difficult to create a cycle of readings parallel to the other three.

Many other Christian denominations have, with some adaptations, adopted our lectionary, which has been a great boon to ecumenism. Today it is not uncommon to find Christians of different traditions sharing their faith over a common set of liturgical Scriptures.

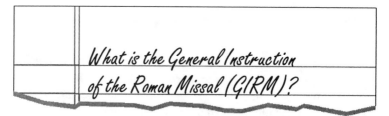

What is the General Instruction of the Roman Missal (GIRM)?

The *General Instruction of the Roman Missal* is the introduction to the sacramentary. It is a pastoral instruction on how to celebrate the Mass. Every sacramental ritual has a similar instruction, which in Latin are called the *praenotanda*. The GIRM as well as the *Introduction to the Lectionary* and the *General Norms for the Liturgical Year and the Calendar* and the ritual texts themselves make up what is considered to be universal liturgical law. These "laws" have the same weight and authority as the *Code of Canon Law*.

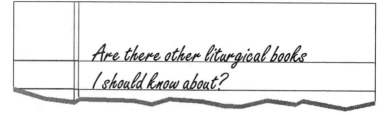

Are there other liturgical books I should know about?

If you are in a leadership position in your parish (for example, a liturgy committee or parish council member or a regular liturgical minister or a catechist), you will want to become familiar with the basic liturgical documents. It may take some time to read through all of them, but you can make it part of a study session at your committee or training meetings.

The most important document is the *Constitution on the Sacred Liturgy* from the Second Vatican Council. This is the cornerstone of the entire liturgical reform. Everything we do liturgically must be in accord with the *Constitution*.

In addition, you will want to read the introductions to the sacramentary and the lectionary.

Even if you are not a musician or on the environment committee, you will benefit from reading *Music in Catholic Worship, Liturgical Music Today,* and *Environment and Art in Catholic Worship.* These three short documents give a clear and basic understanding about liturgy in the U.S. church. These three will answer many of the "Why do we do it this way?" questions you often hear.

If you work with children, read the *Directory for Masses with Children.* If you are looking for insights into better preaching, you will want to read *Fulfilled in Your Hearing,* the U.S. bishops' excellent guide to preparing homilies.

Everybody in the parish will eventually become familiar with the basics of the *Rite of Christian Initiation of Adults.* Parish leaders will want to go beyond the basics. This is a lengthy document and can be difficult to understand. You may want to sponsor a speaker for your committee or a parish education day to go over this. If you work with any of the initiation sacraments—baptism, confirmation, first communion—you need to read this document cover to cover.

In addition, if you work with any of the other sacraments or with funerals, you need to read those ritual books and their introductions, which offer valuable pastoral notes about the meaning of each rite and how to use it.

Eucharist

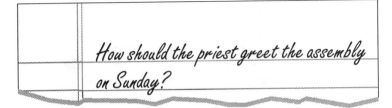

How should the priest greet the assembly on Sunday?

All greetings are ritual greetings. So when we say, "How are you?" or "How's it going?" we expect a reply like "Fine." We expect it because the exchange always happens that way. When it does not happen that way, we feel uncomfortable. For example, the following exchange is both unexpected and unwelcome:

> "How's it going?"
> "Who wants to know?"

In the Mass, there is a formal greeting by the presider and a response by the assembly.

> "The Lord be with you."
> "And also with you."

This greeting seems to have lost some meaning for assemblies—or at least presiders—these days. In many parishes a follow-up greeting is heard immediately after.

> "Good morning."
> "Good morning, Father."

There can be no good reason for this double greeting. The second greeting can only mean one of the following.

> a. The presider did not really mean the first greeting. That is, he did not really mean for the Lord to be with the assembly. Nor did he believe they meant for the Lord to also be with him. Therefore, he said what he really meant, which was that the assembly have a morning that was not unpleasant.

> b. The presider did mean the first greeting, but did not think the assembly believed him. So to show them he was really sincere, he added a second greeting, as if to strengthen the first one.

c. The presider did mean the first greeting and knew the assembly believed he meant it, but he thought the second greeting was more casual and therefore more intimate than the first. The more casual, intimate greeting showed he really cared.

This final possibility for giving a double greeting is perhaps the most likely, but it is also the least justifiable. To say "Good morning" is no less formal than "The Lord be with you" in that both are ritual greetings with patterned responses. We all know what the reply to "Good morning" is going to be. If we do not get that reply, we are uncomfortable and put out.

"Good morning" is also less intimate than "The Lord be with you." Compare the literal meaning of the two greetings and it is obvious the liturgical greeting is a far deeper and more personal invitation. In addition, a relatively small number of people understand the full meaning of "The Lord be with you" and know the ritual reply. It is not exactly a secret handshake, but it does identify us as Christian. In that sense, too, it is more intimate than the secular greeting used in the common transactions of the world.

None of this, however, is reason enough for sticking with, and only with, "The Lord be with you" on Sunday. We use "The Lord be with you. And also with you" because we are about to begin a very powerful action. To celebrate the Mass is to approach the one who dwells in unapproachable light. Without the spirit of the Lord within us as we take on this awesome duty, we would surely die. To greet each other in the prescribed ritual way is to remind ourselves of that fact.

What are the Introductory Rites?

The Introductory Rites are everything from the very beginning of Mass up to and including the opening prayer. The purpose of the Introductory Rites is to bring us together as a community and get us ready to hear the Word of God. This is a clear and simple purpose.

Unfortunately, the rites in the post-Vatican II liturgy are not well designed to carry it out.

The biggest problem is the Introductory Rites are too long. It is possible to have a gathering song, sign of the cross, apostolic greeting, informal greeting, confession of sins, Kyrie, Gloria, and an opening prayer—all in preparation for hearing the Word. We have, by this point, already heard far too many "words." In addition, the Kyrie and the Gloria are properly songs and lose something if merely recited. Yet the musical overload of three songs (when you add the gathering song) in so short a space is too much to bear regularly.

Perhaps the most disruptive element in the Introductory Rites is the penitential rite. The reforms of the Second Vatican Council expanded the penitential rite and made it part of the assembly's prayer. In the time before the Council, the priest and the server recited the Confiteor at the foot of the altar, but it was a private prayer not meant for the general assembly.

The Kyrie, an ancient part of the liturgy, was not and is not intended to be penitential in nature. However, our modern under-standing of the word "mercy" along with the Kyrie's juxtaposition with the Confiteor has transposed it into a penitential prayer. It is, instead, supposed to be a proclamation of praise for the mercy or love God has shown us in Christ.

However, even though ancient, the Kyrie was not originally part of the Introductory Rites either. It was moved there perhaps in the fifth century after the prayer of the faithful had died out in the liturgy. The response to the prayer of the faithful had been *Kyrie eleison* or "Lord have mercy." Now that the prayer of the faithful has been restored to the liturgy, the retention of the Kyrie in the Introductory Rites creates an odd redundancy.

Neither was the Gloria part of the original Introductory Rites; it came into the liturgy perhaps by the sixth century. But it was used only on festive occasions and *only* when the bishop presided. It was not until after the eleventh century that the Gloria came to be used at ordinary parish liturgies.

The gathering song and the opening prayer are the two most important parts of the Introductory Rites. The gathering song is the key element for accomplishing the stated purposed of the Introduc-tory Rites: "to make the assembled people a unified community and to prepare them properly to listen to God's word and celebrate the Eucharist" (*General Instruction of the Roman Missal* 24). It should "create an atmosphere of celebration. It helps put the assembly in the proper frame of mind for listening to the Word of God. It helps people to become conscious of themselves as a worshiping community" (*Music in Catholic Worship* 61). By joining our voices in one song, we become the unified community so that we can properly hear God's Word. It is important, therefore, that the song is one everybody knows well—even by heart.

The opening prayer is what puts us in the presence of the Lord and articulates our relationship as a people dependent upon God's grace. It is the climax of the Introductory Rites. The older name for the opening prayer is the "collect." It was given this name because with this prayer the presider "collects" all the prayer and praise that has gone before and presents it to God as we ready ourselves to hear God's Word.

The U.S. bishops are studying possible revisions in the Introductory Rites that would allow for more flexibility and simplification on most Sundays.

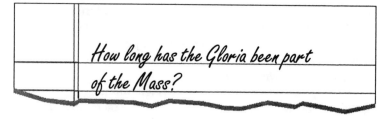

How long has the Gloria been part of the Mass?

The Gloria is a song of praise based on the hymn of the angels in Luke 2:14, which resembles the Psalms in structure and style. The basic structure of the modern Gloria has been around since at least the fourth century and can be found in several different versions from that era. It seems to have first found its way into the divine office (Liturgy of the Hours) in the Syrian and Byzantine rite churches by the fifth century. In the western church, the Gloria was seen as a thanksgiving song or a festival song, not as a liturgical song. Not until the sixth century was there any record of the Gloria being part of the Roman Eucharist. Even then, however, the Gloria could be sung only at a Mass at which a bishop presided. Those liturgies were likely to be "festivals" or great feasts, and the Gloria seemed appropriate in that context. By the end of the eleventh century, the restriction of the Gloria to Masses with bishops had faded. The current practice of singing it on Sundays and feast days outside Advent and Lent became universal in the western church. The Gloria never became part of the eucharistic liturgy in the churches of the eastern rites, however.

From the outset, it seems clear the Gloria was meant to be a song of the assembly. However, this probably died out quickly because Masses at which bishops presided would not have been a regular occurrence for the laity, and they would have had few opportunities to learn the text and tune. (Remember there were no worship aids or pew hymnals until long after the invention of the printing press.) Also, because of the festive nature of the liturgies at which the bishops presided, the people preferred the more elaborate settings a choir could perform.

The reform of the Second Vatican Council emphasized the need for the assembly to play a more active role in the liturgy. The bishops therefore called for a new poetic and singable translation so that the assembly might again give voice to this ancient hymn of praise.

Finally, it is important to emphasize the Gloria is a song. As such, make every effort to sing the Gloria—even if in a simple chant—instead of merely reciting it.

> *Our parish usually doesn't do the responsorial psalm listed in the missalette. Is it okay to change the psalm?*

The psalm between the readings is supposed to be an authentic response of the assembly to the Word of God. To accomplish this, the entire system of psalmody was revised by the commission that revised the lectionary after the Second Vatican Council. Individual psalms were chosen to reflect the mood and spirit of the first reading and, in a sense, complete it. The verses of the responsorial psalms were set in stanzas of equal length so singing them would be easier. The refrain of the psalm, meant to be sung by the entire assembly, is the summation of the meaning of the psalm. It is the explanation of the entire piece.

Because these psalms were chosen so carefully, a parish will want to replace the chosen psalm only for a very good reason. And, in most parishes today, a very good reason exists. That is the fact that we do not know very many psalms well enough to sing them. As a pastoral compromise, the liturgical rubrics allow for the choice of a seasonal psalm to facilitate the singing of the assembly. Perhaps after a couple of generations Catholics will know enough psalmody that we can enthusiastically sing the psalm of the day. Some parishes have already reached this point.

If the psalm of the day is so important, wouldn't it be better to recite the chosen psalm instead of singing a different one?

To understand why singing a seasonal psalm is a better option than reciting the psalm of the day, we have to remember the purpose of the psalm. The responsorial psalm is our enthusiastic response to the saving Word of God (*Music in Catholic Worship* 63). Ritually, this demands a sung response. Singing involves more of ourselves. Singing requires energy. It also requires something of a commitment and a sacrifice. Traditionally, when something is really important, we sing about it. For example, we sing the "Star Spangled Banner," "Happy Birthday," and school fight songs. Most commercials include singing because the advertiser wants us to know his or her product is worth singing about. So singing is the priority. The responsorial psalm is spoken only on rare occasions. Even at weekday Masses, most assemblies can learn a few simple psalm chants that can be sung a capella.

> *Our pastor wants to get rid of the missalettes so people will look at the lector during the readings. But the lectors read so poorly we can't understand the words without a printed copy. Why can't we keep the missalettes?*

The Word of God is the foundation of our faith and the way in which we bring others to faith. Both you and your pastor have the same concern: How do we make the Word of God as clear and compelling as possible? Obviously, if the lector cannot be heard or understood, the next best thing is to have an aid to read along with. But it is only "next best."

If the lector can be heard and understood, reading along *diminishes* the communication of the Word. Our bodies, tone of voice, facial expression, and gestures all communicate information. The Word of God is a living Word, not simply a text. To communicate the Word as fully as possible, it is necessary to use all our human, bodily powers of communication. If the lector cannot make eye contact with the people he or she is trying to communicate with, his or her efforts are diminished.

This obviously means there is more to proclamation than just being heard and understood. Good lectors move beyond the basic skills of public speaking to a higher level of communication. Good lectors communicate their faith to the assembly. It is only by communicating their faith in the Word that they can move others to faith in the Word. Good lectors never think in terms of "doing a reading." They think in terms of changing hearts. Lectors will have a hard time changing hearts if all the eyes of the assembly are buried in books, reading along word for word.

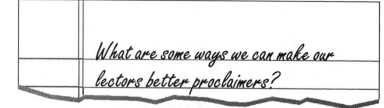

What are some ways we can make our lectors better proclaimers?

Not everyone has the gift to be a lector. But almost everyone can read clearly in public. There is no trick to this and not much skill. It simply takes practice. A liturgy committee or pastor has to be unyielding in demanding that lectors practice. Reading over the Scripture in the sacristy ten minutes before Mass is not practice. Practice means reading aloud several times a day for several days at a minimum. If every lector put in this basic amount of practice, the quality of reading would improve dramatically.

But usually, this will still not be lectoring. That is, it would not be the kind of proclamation that can change hearts. To do that, lectors need to take a second step. They need to pray. They need to pray about the reading and with the reading. They need to discover, through prayer, the single most important point God is asking them to make through that particular reading. Then they need to shape their reading so that it focuses on that point.

Not everyone can do this. To do it well is a talent and a gift of the Spirit. A pastor's or liturgy committee's first task is to get all the lectors to be good public speakers. Then, through their own prayer, they help the lectors discern who of them is called to be a lector and who would best serve the parish in another ministry.

Lectoring is not a right or a privilege. It is a ministry that helps bring people to faith. It is the power of God's Spirit that calls us all to use our gifts for that mission. Some are called to lector, but most are not. The community is best served when those with a true gift for lectoring proclaim the Word and those who are merely good public speakers discern where their true ministry lies.

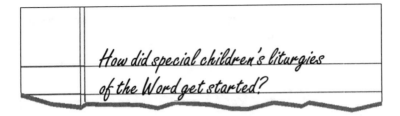

How did special children's liturgies of the Word get started?

In 1973 the Congregation for Divine Worship published the *Directory for Masses with Children*. The overall aim of the document is to provide direction for adapting the liturgy in such a way that children can participate fully, consciously, and actively. In chapter two of that document, the writers give guidance for a typical Sunday liturgy in which "a good many children take part along with the large number of adults." The document says that care should be taken that children do not feel neglected and that some account should be taken of their presence. Article 17 reads:

> Sometimes, moreover, if the place itself and the nature of the community permit, it will be appropriate to celebrate the liturgy of the word, including a homily, with the children in a separate, but not too distant, room. Then, before the eucharistic liturgy begins, the children are led to the place where the adults have meanwhile celebrated their own liturgy of the word.

In the last decade, this provision has been used more often. It is now the case that many parishes *regularly* dismiss children from the main worship space for their own Liturgy of the Word. There is some dispute about the wisdom of this. The document seems to indicate that this would be an occasional practice and not the rule. We have to wonder about the liturgical formation of children who are raised up in a regular worship experience that is not the experience of the larger community. Nevertheless, in those places where the children's Liturgy of the Word is done well, it can lead to greater participation by the children.

It is important to remember that the permission given in the document is for the children to be dismissed to continue the celebration of the *liturgy*. This is to be in no way a catechetical session or recreation. It is to be a liturgical experience that is at least as full as that in the main worship space. There should be music, singing, gesture, liturgical posture, and the use of robust liturgical symbols.

A homily is always to be given, and the liturgy is to take place in a worthy environment.

Where should homilists preach from?

Ideally, homilists would preach from the ambo. This is not a hard and fast rule, but it makes sense. Since the reform of the Second Vatican Council, it is much clearer to us that the homily is part of the Liturgy of the Word. We spent much catechetical energy in the 1960s and 1970s teaching people that there should not be two lecterns, one for the lector and another for the priest. The Word is a unit, we said, and it is ideally all proclaimed from the same place.

The homily is part and parcel of that same Word. Preaching the homily from the ambo gives it a ritual stature that says it is part of the Word.

Sometimes preachers want to move out from behind the ambo to feel more intimate with the assembly. This is a good goal, but it doesn't always work. In many worship spaces, if preachers move off the altar platform down to the same floor level of the assembly, they immediately become less accessible to and less intimate with most of the assembly. They simply cannot be seen and so become a disembodied voice floating over the sound system. The preachers may feel more connected, as will those who sit in the front of the church; however, the back-row-Catholics, those most likely to need a stronger connection with the church, will feel even less connected to an invisible preacher than to an ambo-restricted one.

If the homilists believe they are not close enough to the people when they preach, it may that the ambo was poorly designed in the first place. The Gospel should feel as direct and intimate as the homily does. A felt need to move closer says the ambo might be too remote.

Still, there may be times when the style of the homily calls for a preacher to move away from the ambo. If preachers can minimize these times, the impact will be greater on the few occasions they do preach from another place.

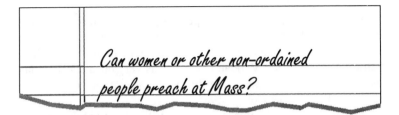

Can women or other non-ordained people preach at Mass?

A distinction needs to be made here between preaching in general and preaching a homily. Only a priest or a deacon can preach a homily at Mass.

However, all Christians are called to preach the Good News of salvation in Christ. We preach through our words and through our example. At times, some non-ordained Christians are called on to preach in a formal way in a public setting. This might be a Christian meeting or retreat or it might be part of a faith-sharing session.

At liturgies other than Mass at which lay people preside, the presider is encouraged to preach in much the same way and for the same reasons that an ordained presider preaches: to encourage the faith of the worshiping assembly. Such liturgies include Sunday celebrations at which an ordained priest is absent, Liturgy of the Hours, and, in some places, weddings, baptisms, and funerals.

What, then, is the distinction between preaching in general and preaching a homily? The simplest explanation is that a homily is the preaching a priest or deacon does during a liturgy. It is a homily, and not general preaching, because an ordained minister does it.

This may seem a little nit-picky, but it goes to the heart of what it means to be ordained. When we ask if a non-ordained person can give a homily, it is similar to asking if a non-ordained person can pray the eucharistic prayer. Any of us can pray the prayer to ourselves. In fact, we pray it every Sunday *with* the priest. We could even pray it aloud in a public meeting of Christians, as on a retreat or in a faith-sharing group, for spiritual or catechetical reasons. In addition, the official rite for Sunday celebrations in the absence of a priest includes a prayer of thanksgiving as part of the ritual. However, even though any of us can pray the eucharistic prayer, it is not, in fact, a eucharistic prayer unless a priest prays it in the context of a celebration of the Eucharist.

Likewise with a homily, it is not a homily unless it is preached by a priest or deacon in the midst of a Christian liturgy.

So, then, can a non-ordained person preach at Mass if we just don't call it a homily? Perhaps on rare occasions there might be a reason to do so, but such preaching cannot supplant the homily. The reform of the Second Vatican Council was very clear that Sunday Mass is to always include a homily and it is strongly recommended for other liturgies as well.

The clear reason for this is the intimate link between the Liturgy of the Word and the Liturgy of the Eucharist. The one who will break the bread does so as the one who breaks open the Word. It is the sacramental role of the priest to call the community to conversion and faith through the Word and through the Eucharist. When that ritual link is broken by the introduction of another preacher (even if it is another priest!) the ritual is weakened and the connection between Word and Eucharist becomes less clear. In a sense, we begin to treat the Word as if it is some separate thing that we do during the first half of the Mass, and when that is done, we move on to do the Eucharist. It is not separate, and we cannot treat it as such.

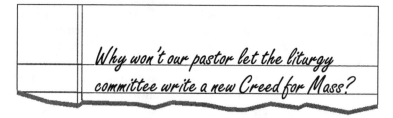

Why won't our pastor let the liturgy committee write a new Creed for Mass?

Sometimes liturgy committee members think the words of the Creed tend to become routine and boring. It is understandable that they want to do something to liven it up and make it more interesting to the assembly. But the Creed dates from the very early church. It has been the statement of faith for Christians for almost two thousand years. There is nothing wrong with trying to find new ways of expressing our faith, but in the liturgy we are saying not only "This is what we believe" but also "This is what the church believes." And the church includes all those Christians who prayed that same prayer for all those centuries.

A more effective way to inject new vigor into the Creed and into any of the prayers of the Mass is to get a small group together and read the prayer aloud. Then ask the group, "What did you see?"

Keep the group literal and focused. Do not let them wander off into what the prayer "means." What are the visual images in the prayer? Then read the prayer again and ask, "What did you hear?" Read the prayer a final time and ask, "What will this cost?" Again, get very concrete. Ask each person, "If you were to take the prayer seriously, how would your life be changed?" The next time that prayer is prayed in the liturgy, it will be as if it were a brand new prayer.

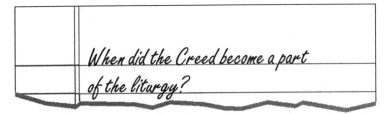

When did the Creed become a part of the liturgy?

"C reed" comes from the Latin word *credo*, which means "I believe." The first credal statements were part of the baptismal rite and were very simple, such as the classic New Testament phrase: "Jesus is Lord." These simple creeds eventually developed into what we now call the Apostles' Creed. This creed is still used at baptisms, usually in a question-and-answer format.

In the fourth century there was a church council in Nicea and another in Constantinople (much like the Second Vatican Council). The Council of Nicea defined some important aspects of our faith, and these faith statements were later fashioned into a creed at another council in Constantinople. It is that Creed, called the Nicene Creed, which we now usually say at Mass. But it was not at first intended for use in the Mass.

Not until the latter half of the fifth century was the creed first used in the liturgy. That took place in Antioch. In the next century, the Creed was used in the Mass at Constantinople and then in Spain. In Spain, the Creed served as a sort of test for a prevalent group of heretics called the Arians. The Creed was recited just before the fraction rite. Any Arians present would not be able to truly recite everything in the Creed and so could not come to communion. From there, the use of the Creed in the Mass spread throughout Europe. However, Rome still maintained the more ancient practice of not reciting the Creed in the Mass.

In 1014, Henry II visited Rome and was shocked to learn the Creed was not said in the liturgy. (You can almost hear him saying, "But that's the way we've always done it.") He prevailed upon Pope Benedict VIII to make the addition. Some commentators note that the fact that Henry's army was camped just outside the city didn't diminish his influence any.

In the Roman Rite, the Creed is said as a response to the Liturgy of the Word "as a way for the people to respond and to give assent to the word of God heard in the readings and through the homily and for them to call to mind the truths of faith before they begin to celebrate the eucharist" (*General Instruction of the Roman Missal* 43). From this definition of purpose it is clear why the liturgy was "creedless" for more than a thousand years. Responding to the Word in faith is exactly the purpose of the Liturgy of the Eucharist. The Creed simply repeats what is already proclaimed in the eucharistic prayer and lived out in communion.

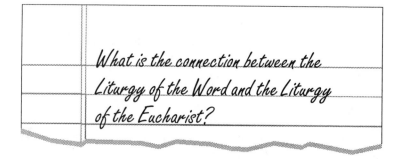

What is the connection between the Liturgy of the Word and the Liturgy of the Eucharist?

The Liturgy of the Word is the first half of the Mass, and it concludes with the Creed and the prayer of the faithful. The Liturgy of the Eucharist is the second half of the Mass, which begins with the collection and preparation of gifts. Because of the way ritual works, the connection between the two is important. In the ritual of the Mass, we enter into the story of Jesus' life, death, and resurrection. By ritualizing that story, we become part of it and Jesus becomes part of us.

We know that Jesus is the Word of God. We also know that all creation flows from the Word of God. In the beginning, when God spoke, creation happened. The Word of God—Jesus—is the agent of creation.

When we proclaim the Word of God in our Sunday assembly, we are participating in that same creative action. The Word—which is Jesus—is present and creative. What gets created is faith. Those with no faith receive faith. Those with faith receive a deepening of faith. That creation of faith happens every Sunday at Mass.

Faith demands a response. It is impossible to receive faith and not respond to it. Our ritual response is to stand and gather around the table. At the table, ritually, we take, bless, break, and share the bread of life. Likewise, we take, bless, pour, and share the cup of salvation. These are ritual actions that remind us of the actions in Jesus' life and make those actions present. Jesus was often sharing meals. But more significantly, he shared himself, being broken on the cross just as he is broken in the bread and poured out in the cup.

This action of the Eucharist is a direct result of the faith we receive from Jesus, the Word. The ritual connection is essential.

However, we cannot stop there. Everything we believe in and celebrate is to be taken out into the world and lived out. In that way we preach the Word in our daily lives. And that Word is creative, as God's Word always is. God's Word creates faith, causing those we encounter to want to respond. They respond by joining us on Sunday to celebrate their faith and to continue the cycle.

In this way we carry on the mission Jesus left us: to evangelize the world.

How should we handle second collections?

Liturgy might be better overall if we did far fewer second collections. The budgets of numerous national, diocesan, and parish projects have come to count on second collections for survival. However, an overdose of second collections makes the liturgy seem like a collection agency for every good idea in need of funding. Second collections foster weak financial planning, and they clutter the liturgy.

Parish leaders might begin to look at second collections from the point of view of the assembly. It is not uncommon to have a second collection once or twice a month in many parishes. It is possible to have a second collection every Sunday of the year. Add to this the car washes, raffle tickets, pancake breakfasts, and candy bar sales and the average parishioner begins to see Sunday primarily as the time when the parish is going to ask for more money. An honest case can be made for expecting Christians to support financially the mission of the church. So make it; ask for pledges once a year, and get on with it. Avoid turning Sunday into a telethon.

So what to do about the collections mandated by national and diocesan organizations? One solution is to build these costs into the regular parish operating budget. That may mean some decrease in the amount of money available for other expenses in the parish, but that is no different from the reality all our parishioners live with when a national organization (like the government) requires them to contribute something out of their household budgets.

In addition, expand the use of special envelopes in the boxes of envelopes distributed to parishes each fiscal year. These envelopes can be dropped into the regular collection and sorted by the money counters. Extra envelopes can be placed in the pews for non-envelope contributors to use. Every special collection can be planned far enough ahead that these envelopes can be added into the mix.

If a second collection must be taken up for some reason, there are a couple of ways to do it that can ease the disruption to the liturgy. The first is to have double the usual number of ushers and collection baskets available. When the first group of ushers taking up the usual collection finishes collecting from the first three or four rows, the second crew begins the second collection. This delays the liturgy only minimally. A second option is to have ushers with collection baskets standing at the exits as people leave.

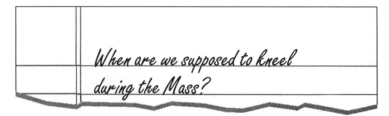

When are we supposed to kneel during the Mass?

The place to find the directives for posture at Mass is the *General Instruction of the Roman Missal* (GIRM), which can be found in the front of the sacramentary. Article 21 reads in part:

> Unless other provision is made, at every Mass the people should stand from the beginning of the entrance song...to the end of the opening prayer or collect; for the singing of the *Alleluia* before the gospel; while the gospel is proclaimed; during the profession of faith and the general intercessions; from the prayer over the gifts to the end of the Mass, except at the places indicated later in this paragraph. They should sit during the readings before the gospel and during the responsorial psalm, for the homily and the presentation of the gifts, and, if this seems helpful, during the silence after communion. They should kneel at the consecration unless prevented by lack of space, the number of people present, or some other good reason.

According to this directive, the only time we would kneel at Mass is during the consecration. However, the GIRM goes on to say that local bishops' conferences may adapt these postures. In an appendix to the GIRM, the U.S. bishops added the following directive that the assembly should kneel not just for the consecration but for the entire eucharistic prayer (from after the Holy to after the Great Amen).

Although it is not strictly legal, these postures often get changed in local parishes in the following ways:

1. Some parishes will kneel for the penitential rite during Lent.

2. Some parishes will stand for the eucharistic prayer either for the Easter season or throughout the year.

3. Almost all parishes kneel after the Lamb of God and after receiving communion.

The departure from the rubrics that seems to cause the most upset is the second. Many people find standing during the eucharistic prayer to be a more prayerful posture for making such a powerful statement of faith. Others see kneeling as a sign of deep respect for the action of the prayer and the presence of Christ in the eucharistic elements. What is most disheartening about the debate over which is "correct" is the attitude that one side or the other is being unfaithful, disrespectful, reactionary, or intransigent. Both postures have historical precedence. It is difficult to imagine any Christian assuming a posture of prayer with the express purpose of being irreverent.

More troubling is the lack of debate over the third deviation. Almost every parish kneels during the communion rite (after the Lamb of God and after receiving communion) when we should be standing at the ready to first share in the Eucharist and then spread it into the world. This is clearly a moment that requires an erect and alert assembly. The rubrics indicate this as does the history of the Mass.

It is appropriate to kneel during the eucharistic prayer and perhaps during the penitential rite at Mass, but no other time.

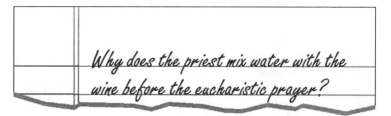

Why does the priest mix water with the wine before the eucharistic prayer?

This practice comes from the early middle eastern culture where the liturgy originated. It was the custom at the time to dilute strong wine so it would not be too strong to drink. The cultural practice simply carried over into the liturgy with little thought or meaning. Over time, people began to ascribe meaning to the practice. One of the common understandings was the idea that mixing water and wine represented the water and blood flowing from Jesus' side when he was crucified. However, the ritual has little actual significance and can be done at a side table instead of at the altar.

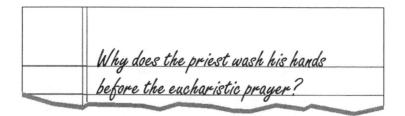

Why does the priest wash his hands before the eucharistic prayer?

The actual origins are unclear. In the beginning, the ritual would have taken place after the gifts were received. In the early church, the gifts would have included many different foods along with the bread and wine. In addition, the gifts were incensed as is still done sometimes today. The presider's hands may have been dirty after all this, and washing may have been needed. However, early cultures did not understand germs the way we do, and the hand washing may have been simply a symbolic gesture of inward cleansing instead. The current understanding of the ritual is ambiguous and it is a minor part of the liturgy.

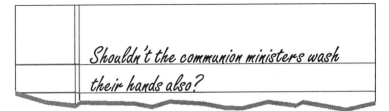

Shouldn't the communion ministers wash their hands also?

No. We presume communion ministers come to church with clean hands or wash them once they get there. Adding another hand washing to the liturgy is an unnecessary accretion and takes the focus away from the primary action of the Mass.

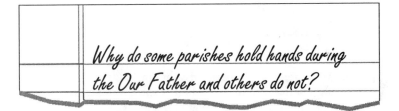

Why do some parishes hold hands during the Our Father and others do not?

Holding hands during the Lord's Prayer is a spontaneous practice that has sprung up in some communities. It is not part of the official rite, and it is not being promoted by any leadership group. It remains to be seen if it will take hold as a Catholic practice or if it will eventually lose its novelty and die out.

There are some problems with the practice ritually and theologically. One of the significant reforms of the Second Vatican Council was to eliminate useless repetitions. When you ask people why they like to hold hands during the Lord's Prayer, they will usually talk about the sense of unity it creates. However, this is the express purpose of communion. The gesture also seems a duplication of the sign of peace—another gesture of clasping hands—which immediately follows it.

However, those parishes that do hold hands during the Lord's Prayer are quite fond of the practice. Unlike when we first started doing the sign of peace, these parishes are not holding hands just because they think church authorities are telling them they have to. They are doing it out of a genuine desire to connect in a visible way with those around them.

As a general rule, this is probably not a practice to be encouraged in places where it is not currently being done. Likewise, it is not a practice that ought to be suppressed where it seems to have become a genuine part of the people's prayer.

> *Why do we shake hands with each other at the sign of peace when we have already done so at the beginning of Mass? It seems redundant.*

There is a difference between greeting one another before Mass and exchanging the sign of peace before the communion rite. The greeting that some parishes do just before Mass is not part of the ritual. It is a way to loosen people up a little and help at least get to know the name of the person next to them before celebrating together. The sign of peace, on the other hand, is an ancient ritual that had been part of the liturgy in the early church and was lost for a while. The ritual was recovered by the Second Vatican Council. The placement of the sign of peace has varied over the centuries. In the very earliest tradition, the sign of peace came at the end of the intercessions and was an enactment of Matthew 5:23-24 ("If you bring your gift to the altar, and there recall that your brother has anything against you, leave your gift there at the altar, go first and be reconciled with your brother, and then come and offer your gift."). In the fourth century, the intercessions became simply a litany of praise (which was later moved to the beginning of Mass and became the Kyrie). Perhaps for that reason, the sign of peace was moved to just before communion, where it is currently.

Because of its connection with Matthew 5:23-24, there was a time when only those who were receiving communion would exchange the sign of peace. Soon, that meant only the clergy were exchanging the peace because only the clergy were receiving communion at most liturgies. In the fifteenth century, this restriction was lifted so all could share in the sign of peace. However, by that time the sign of peace had become so linked with the clergy that the exchange was seen as coming *from* the presider and handed down to the assembly. This misunderstanding of the gesture was exacerbated by the use, especially in England, of the pax-board, an ornamented plaque which the presider kissed and passed down to the lower ranks of clergy, who kissed it and then passed the "kiss" on to the rest assembly. This "ranking" of the worshiping body contradicted the unity the gesture was meant to effect.

The use of a pax-board was provided for in the Missal of Pius V of 1570 for high Masses, but in most places the sign of peace had died out by this time. The sign of peace was restored to the liturgy by the reforms of the Second Vatican Council. In the proposed revision of the sacramentary, parishes will have the option of keeping the sign of peace where it is now or moving it to its more ancient position at the end of the intercessions.

The meaning of the ritual is one of reconciliation and unity with each other before either approaching the altar with our gifts or approaching to receive communion. It has a symbolism that is profound. The greeting at the beginning of Mass, on the other hand, is simply a greeting. It means just about the same thing as greeting someone who is passing by on the street. So while the actions may look similar, they are very different. Perhaps it would help if we completely recovered the ritual of what is officially called the "Kiss of Peace." In the ancient Middle East, where Christianity was born, the members of the assembly did actually kiss one another instead of shaking hands as most of us do. We may never feel that comfortable, but kissing during the Peace would distinguish it from the "good morning" before Mass.

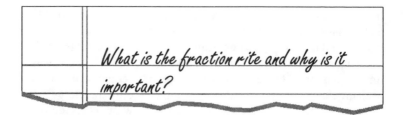

What is the fraction rite and why is it important?

T he fraction rite is the ritual of breaking the bread and pouring the wine for communion. This is one of the central moments of the liturgy, but it is too often lost in a hubbub of activity.

This ritual was originally the source of the name of Mass. The early Christians referred to Sunday worship as "The Breaking of the Bread." Like the disciples on the road to Emmaus, they believed Christ was revealed in "the breaking of the bread."

The bread, the Body of Christ, is broken—just as the Body of Christ was broken on the cross. The wine, the blood of Christ, is poured out—just as the blood of Christ was poured out on the cross. In this breaking we see the life and death of Jesus. In this pouring we are reminded of all the life and death we have experienced and all the life and death that all Christians throughout history have experienced. At this moment we "see" Jesus—not only in the bread broken and cup poured but also in the lives and struggles of the whole Christian communion.

To do the breaking of the bread in such a way to make this symbolism self-evident, we first need bread that can be broken. We need real bread, freshly baked, and lots of it. We need to take the time to break the bread into pieces, perhaps seeing the hardships that have broken apart the lives of all the farmers, harvesters, shippers, millers, bakers, and helpers that went into creating the bread.

We also need rich wine, fragrant and fruitful. We pour out the lives of all the growers, vintners, and distributors that went into creating the wine. We see our own lives poured out as well.

The breaking of the bread is diminished if it is obscured by an overly long sign of peace or the moving of dishes around the altar by assisting ministers. Ideally, everything stops and all hearts and minds become focused on this powerful moment. The presider raises a loaf for all to see and breaks it in half. At that moment, the singing of the Lamb of God begins. When the first loaf has been torn, then the communion ministers can move closer to the altar to help with the breaking and pouring.

Having witnessed Christ—and ourselves—broken apart and poured out, we come to the table to become one again. Christ becomes one in us, and we become one in him.

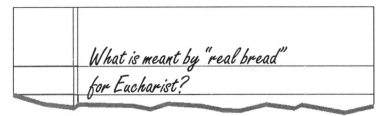

What is meant by "real bread" for Eucharist?

Real bread is bread that looks like food. It does not have to be explained so children will know what it is. The *General Instruction of the Roman Missal* (GIRM) says of the bread for Eucharist: "The nature of the sign demands that the material of the eucharistic celebration appear as actual food" (283). However, the GIRM also says that, according the tradition of the Latin Church, the bread must be unleavened and must be made of only wheat and water. These seem like contradictory directives. It is difficult to imagine unleavened bread made of only wheat and water that looks and tastes like real food. Forced to choose between these two directives, most parishes choose to distribute the pressed wafers most of us grew up with. However, this can hardly satisfy the demand "that the bread appear as actual food." No one would ever confuse the wafers from Mass with anything we would eat otherwise.

Pastoral ministers and liturgy planners will want to ask themselves what they are trying to do at Mass with the choice of bread they make. If they are trying do what Jesus did, real bread is the obvious choice. Jesus used the bread of the table. He used the bread that was easily recognized by all as bread. Jesus used real bread. And while it is theologically possible to have "real presence" when the bread is not quite real, it seems much clearer that real bread better helps the assembly perceive real presence.

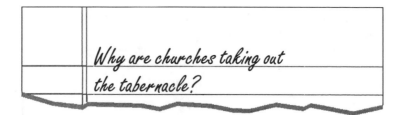

Why are churches taking out the tabernacle?

W hile it may seem that way sometimes, no churches are removing the tabernacle. In accord with the ancient tradition of the church, parishes are again beginning to provide a special place of honor for the tabernacle. This is a practice that has always been the case at the pope's church, St. Peter's Basilica in Rome. There and in most new or renovated churches, the tabernacle is not in the main sanctuary but in a worthy devotional chapel. Some critics see this as disrespectful. They believe church leaders are somehow "pushing Jesus off to the side." Nothing could be further from the truth.

The document *Holy Communion and the Worship of the Eucharist Outside of Mass* states that the respect accorded to the reserved sacrament and adoration by the people "will be achieved more easily if the [tabernacle] chapel is separate from the body of the church" (9). The reasoning is simple. Church buildings are busy places these days. Music rehearsals, wedding rehearsals, decorating for the seasons, putting out worship aids, picking up worship aids, besides all the various liturgies that take place make for a noisy, active worship space. However, adoration of the reserved sacrament is best done in a quiet, meditative space. A separate prayer chapel is a necessity.

In addition, the reforms of the Second Vatican Council recovered for us the distinction between the active and static presences of Christ in the Eucharist. One of the primary reasons for reserving the sacrament (static presence) is to help us remember and lead us back to the celebration of the Eucharist (active presence). To have Christ present in the reserved sacrament at the same time and place we are celebrating Christ's presence in the active sacrament at Mass can be confusing.

When the chief way we participated in the Eucharist was by *watching* instead of sharing in communion, this confusion was not so great. It seemed to many of us the purpose of the Mass was to consecrate the bread regularly so the tabernacle would never be empty so we could adore the real presence of Christ. The purpose of Eucharist, however, is communion in the body, blood, and mission of Christ. Reservation of the sacrament is an important support to that purpose but not the main goal.

To practice a truly Catholic eucharistic piety, it is important for us to provide a place of honor and prayer for the tabernacle and a separate place for the Liturgy of the Eucharist.

> *Why is it that some parishes do not give communion from the tabernacle at Mass anymore?*

It is the action of the entire assembly, presided over by an ordained priest, that makes the celebration of Eucharist an authentic and real experience of Christ. When communion is given from another liturgy to the gathered assembly, the action symbolizes the work of a previous assembly and not the work of the present assembly. The presence of Christ is no different, but the presence of the assembly is different. When we give communion from the tabernacle at Mass, we are saying the work of the present assembly is somehow not full enough and must be supplemented by the work of a previous assembly.

Remember, the purpose of communion is not only the individual reception of holy communion. It is also a bonding and becoming one with the Christ in each other so we can go forth from the liturgy as the body of Christ to do the work of Christ. For that reason, the *General Instruction of the Roman Missal* says:

> It is most desirable that the faithful should receive the body of the Lord in hosts consecrated at the same Mass and should share the cup when it is permitted. Communion is thus a clearer sign of sharing in the sacrifice that is actually being celebrated (56h).

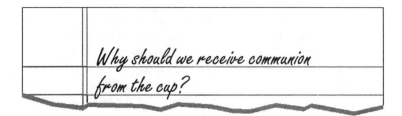

Why should we receive communion from the cup?

The clearest reason is because it is what Jesus asked us to do. Also, as the *General Instruction of the Roman Missal* says, "Holy communion has a more complete form as a sign when it is received under both kinds. For in this manner of reception a fuller light shines on the sign of the eucharistic banquet" (240).

Wine highlights not only the celebratory nature of the paschal mystery but also the suffering and dying. The grapes are crushed and the wine poured out just as Jesus was crushed and his blood poured out.

Some have suggested making the consecrated wine available in individual cups because they are concerned about germs being transmitted. If the ritual involved was a simple case of ingesting the wine, this would not be a problem. But the ritual is more powerful than that. Jesus asked us to drink from the same cup he drank from—a cup of blessing as well as a cup of persecution. If we cannot drink from that same cup, we cannot share in his risen life.

The ideal at Mass is for all to drink from one cup to give witness to our willingness to share in Jesus' cup of blessing and persecution. The size of most of our Sunday assemblies makes this impossible. However, to keep the symbolism as powerful as possible, we want to keep the number of cups we use to a minimum. Providing each person with his or her own cup not only undermines the symbol of the common cup, it also provides a counter-symbol of individual responsibility and achievement. Individualism is an evil to be resisted in worship, not celebrated.

Should the presider receive communion first or last? What about the communion ministers?

This is a fairly new question. For centuries, lay people did not receive communion—at least not very often. Pope Pius X, early in this century, promoted more frequent communion. With the changes brought about by the Second Vatican Council, most Catholics have come to see more of the meal aspects of the Eucharist. And, if Eucharist is a meal to them, it makes sense to them that the host would not eat before the guests.

This perception is something of a carryover from a pre-Vatican II understanding of the Mass. In that era, many Catholics thought of the Mass as something the priest did while the rest of the faithful "attended" or "listened." In a post-Vatican II understanding of the Mass, the presider is not the host of the meal; Jesus is. The presider is as much a guest as the rest of the assembly.

With that in mind, it may not be a bad idea to take the rubric of the sacramentary literally when it says that, after the call to the table and the people's response ("Lord, I am not worthy to receive you..."), the presider "consumes the body of Christ. Next he...drinks the blood of Christ" (*General Instruction of the Roman Missal* [GIRM] 116). The rubrics then direct the presider to take the bread to the communicants to share with them.

Nothing is said of the communion ministers, of course, because there were no communion ministers other than the priest when the GIRM was written. Nevertheless, by the same reasoning that the communion ministers are not "hosts" of the meal or even "assistant hosts," a parish might logically have the communion ministers receive communion at the same time as or just after the presider.

The effect, though, of structuring the communion rite in this way is usually to put the assembly in a passive position—something that is very much against the mandate of the Second Vatican Council. This time becomes a moment when the assembly watches—usually in silence—what the presider and the communion ministers are doing up in the sanctuary. It is too similar to the "ocular communion" of a previous era.

Until we are a few generations beyond the shift caused by the Second Vatican Council, the ritual will be more powerful and more effective if the ritual happens something like this: Immediately after the assembly's "Lord, I am not worthy" response, the communion song begins and the presider and the communion ministers move out to their stations to share the bread and cup. The communion ministers and the presider might then join the ends of the remaining communion lines to receive communion themselves as their own lines diminish.

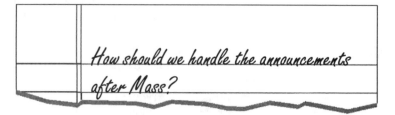

How should we handle the announcements after Mass?

Most often the announcements take place at the end of Mass. When they take place at the end of Mass, they are to be done *after* the prayer after communion. But they do not have to go at the end. A close look at the dynamics of the liturgy shows us the announcements can also take place at the *beginning* of Mass. Liturgists tell us the first action of the liturgy is the gathering of the community. This gathering begins as we enter the parking lot, continues as we walk toward the church, goes on as we enter and find our pew, and flows into the opening song. If just before we sing a minister of hospitality or a "gathering" minister welcomes any visitors and asks us to introduce ourselves to one another, we would consider that to be part of the business of the community at the moment. As a continuation of community business, the gathering minister could call our attention to any particular needs we ought to hold in prayer during the week. He or she could call our attention to any other important community business, such as an upcoming chili supper. All this serves to call and gather us as a particular community concerned about and interested in particular issues. The final act of community business before we are called to prayer is to stand and sing in one voice with one communal heart.

The process goes more smoothly if one person is in charge of prioritizing and editing announcements. Not everything needs to be announced, and someone who is not afraid to say "no" in a tactful way would be a good person to put in charge of the announcements.

The best announcements last no longer than thirty seconds each. That is the length of most television commercials and it is the length of most parishioners' attention spans for advertisements, no matter how worthy.

Requests for announcements are more helpful if written out in full. "Please announce the chili supper" is not as helpful as "The youth group invites all the parishioners of St. Placid's to the annual chili supper this Tuesday night. See the bulletin for details."

Verbal announcements are much more effective when they have a corresponding notice in the Sunday bulletin. That way, the written announcement can list all the details such as time, place, cost, etc. The verbal announcement can be a simple statement that the event or activity is taking place and interested parishioners can see the bulletin for details. Do not bend this rule if someone forgets to put an announcement in the bulletin. "Forgetting" leads to more forgetting if there is always a backup available in the verbal announcements.

Encourage parishioners to make their own announcements. This builds a sense of community and responsibility. (But remember the thirty-second rule.)

Announcements are usually not made by the presider or by the lector. Their jobs are to preside and to proclaim the Word of God. Encourage other members of the community to take on the responsibility of making announcements.

Stewardship campaigns, building campaigns, and other lengthy messages often take place at the time of the announcements. This should happen rarely, four times a year at most. The assembly can be warned there will be a lengthy message coming. Other parts of the liturgy can be streamlined to compensate for the time. Yes, in the ideal world, everyone would be so enthralled with the spirit that an extra ten or twenty minutes listening to the stewardship chairperson talk about the complexities of the parish budget would be no big deal. But it is a big deal, and people feel abused if we do not respect their time. Schedule these rare messages for Sundays in Ordinary Time, which can be more easily abbreviated. The homily can begin or end with the statement, "My homily will be (has been) a little shorter today because Tom from the stewardship committee is going to share a few words with us at the end of Mass." If you regularly have your announcements at the beginning of the liturgy, the announcement on this Sunday could be, "There will be no announcements today, and Father's homily will be a little shorter than usual because the stewardship committee has some important information to share with us after communion."

Last thought: It will be on Mothers' Day on a Sunday in Easter when the 150 First Communicants will all be at the 11:00 a.m. Mass and the Monsignor's retirement party is scheduled for 12:30 that you will have a "priority one" list of about twenty-five announcements. Just take two aspirin, and remember the church will survive in spite of us.

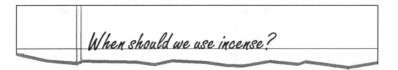

When should we use incense?

Roman Catholics seem to have a love-hate relationship with incense. It is something many of us remember fondly from our childhood. Yet there seems to be much fuss made about it when it is used today.

It is true that some people have allergies to incense. These folks are few in number, but you can count on hearing from some of them every time incense is used. While we can be sensitive to using high-quality incense (it tends to cause less of a problem) and good ventilation, and while we can even warn those parishioners we know have a particular difficulty, we cannot allow a few people to determine the ritual character of our communities. To do so would mean to have no wine because some people react badly to alcohol, no bread because some people have wheat allergies, no Christmas trees because some people do not believe in cutting down live trees for Christmas, no lit candles because some people are overly scrupulous about fire codes, and so on.

So when to use incense? Incense can be used at any liturgy. It probably ought to be used at every Sunday liturgy or at least those considered the primary Sunday Masses. The places for using incense in the Mass listed in the *General Instruction of the Roman*

Missal include during the entrance procession, at the beginning of Mass to incense the altar, as part of the Gospel procession, and at the preparation of the gifts.

The simplest thing to do is to use incense in the opening procession only. It can be used in moderation in this way on the Sundays of ordinary time, using a little more during Advent and Lent, and using it copiously during Christmas and Easter. Easter Vigil should be like worshiping in a cloud.

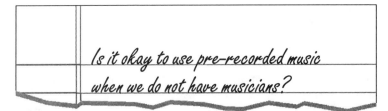

Is it okay to use pre-recorded music when we do not have musicians?

It is difficult to imagine why a parish would want to use pre-recorded music in the liturgy. Music is a form of liturgical prayer. Using pre-recorded music would be akin to using pre-recorded presider's prayers or pre-recorded readings.

Music is the gift of the assembly to God and to each other. We do not want our gift to be someone else's pre-recorded song coming over the speakers. We want it to be the song of the assembly. It would be good if the goal of every assembly was to know enough music by heart that they could make a worthy gift of their voices even when a trained musician was not available to assist them.

The document *Liturgical Music Today* says:

> The liturgy is a complexus of signs expressed by living human beings. Music, being preeminent among those signs, ought to be 'live.' While recorded music, therefore, might be used to advantage outside the liturgy as an aid in the teaching of new music, it should, as a general norm, never be used within the liturgy to replace the congregation, the choir, the organist or other instrumentalist (60).

The document goes on to list three possible exceptions. It says recorded music may be used to accompany an outdoor procession or, when used carefully, in Masses with children. And *occasionally* it might be used during long periods of silence in a communal reconciliation. However, given the previous statement that music is a preeminent sign or symbol in the liturgy, it is difficult to understand why even these exceptions are allowed.

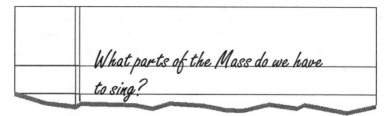

What parts of the Mass do we have to sing?

The liturgy is very much like an opera in the sense that the entire event is meant to be sung. However, no parish has the stamina or the resources to make every Mass, every Sunday, an operatic production. Given that, we need to know what *must* be sung every Sunday.

Music in Catholic Worship lists six types of songs found in the liturgy and lists within those types the examples that ought to be sung even when little else is sung.

> a. Acclamations: Assemblies ought to always sing the gospel acclamation, "Holy, Holy," memorial acclamation, Great Amen, and doxology to the Lord's Prayer. (In actual practice, few parishes sing the doxology to the Lord's Prayer.)

> b. Processional Songs: entrance song, communion procession song. (In the earlier tradition of the church, these songs were psalms. Often, contemporary composers have written melodies for psalms to be used in these places, and we sing them sometimes without realizing we are singing psalmody.) Note the recessional song is not listed as a primary song here.

> c. Responsorial Psalm: This is always sung. This is also an occasion when the cantor or choir may sing "alone" but only on the verses. The assembly should sing at least the refrain. The

assembly also may sing some of the verses, alternating with the cantor or choir.

d. Ordinary Chants: These may be spoken or sung depending upon the solemnity of the season and the nature of the chant. They include the Kyrie, the Gloria, the Lord's Prayer, the Lamb of God, and the Creed. Of these, the Gloria and the Lamb of God are almost always sung in most U.S. parishes at Sunday liturgies.

e. Supplementary Songs: The song during the preparation of gifts ("offertory" song) and the recessional song are supplementary songs. These songs may be used in places where the rite does not list any spoken text or call for any singing but where singing sometimes can enhance the liturgy. These can be sung by the assembly or by the cantor or choir alone. These are the least important songs in the liturgy and would be worked on only after the others have been mastered.

   The song after communion is also listed as a supplementary song. This is not a "meditation" song but rather a "hymn, psalm, or other song of praise...sung by the entire congregation" (*General Instruction of the Roman Missal* 61). This can be an important song in the liturgy, providing a climactic moment for the assembly to proclaim in one voice the joy and unity they have just experienced in communion. In order to work, the song after communion should be a rich, full piece that everyone knows almost by heart. It should express an idea of thanksgiving or joy. And, of course, it is ideally sung standing.

f. Litanies: Besides the Lamb of God, which was already mentioned, litanies include the general intercessions, the litany of saints, and the invocations of Christ in the penitential rite. These can be sung or spoken depending upon the solemnity of the rite. However, litanies are usually more effective when sung.

Is it all right to applaud for the musicians at the end of Mass when they do an especially good job?

To applaud for the musicians implies that they are performers and that we are an audience. In reality, the primary musicians at Mass are the members of the assembly. The people up front (or in the choir loft) are there to assist us with our music.

The question is perhaps easier to understand if it is asked in terms of the homilist, lector, or communion minister. Is it appropriate to applaud for these ministers when they do a good job? Clearly it is not. Likewise, we would not applaud for the musicians, no matter how wonderful they are.

On some occasions, when the liturgy as a whole has been exceptional, it might be appropriate for the assembly to applaud for itself as an acclamation of joy and praise. However, a more liturgical response would be to sing another song if the joy is really so pregnant it cannot be contained.

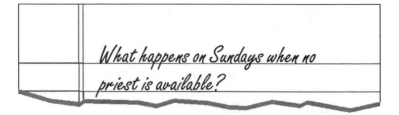

What happens on Sundays when no priest is available?

Because of the growing shortage of ordained priests, many communities experience at least occasional Sundays when no ordained priest is available. People in those parishes might go to another parish for Mass, but often that is not an option. Recently the U.S. bishops published guidelines for celebrating Sunday without an ordained presider. These celebrations are either a Liturgy of the

Word followed by communion or Liturgy of the Hours followed by communion. The service is led by a lay person. It is up to each diocese to set guidelines for how to choose and train these leaders.

Some liturgists have challenged this development. They are worried people might confuse these liturgies with Eucharist because communion is shared. A better option might be to celebrate the Liturgy of the Word or the Liturgy of the Hours without communion.

However, the current situation does force Catholics to answer for themselves several important questions. For example, what is the difference between Eucharist and communion? Can women and lay men be effective leaders of the Sunday assembly? What are the root causes of the priest shortage? What can be done about it?

And the most important question: Are we in danger of losing what it means to be Catholic if we cannot celebrate Eucharist every Sunday?

In those places where Sunday communion services are becoming more and more common, it will be important to celebrate Eucharist as well as possible on the Sundays an ordained presider is able to be with the community. It is important to celebrate Eucharist well so the community will recognize a clear distinction between a communion service and Mass. Some things to pay attention to include using real bread every time Mass is celebrated, making communion from the cup an option at every Mass, making sure the acclamations for the eucharistic prayer are sung, and making the breaking of the bread a highlight of the liturgy. In addition, a community is never to receive previously consecrated bread from the tabernacle at a Mass. It will also be important to make sure the eucharistic prayer is prayed in a powerful, moving way. If these things are done well, they will be clearly missed when a communion service is celebrated, and there will be little confusion between a Mass and a communion service.

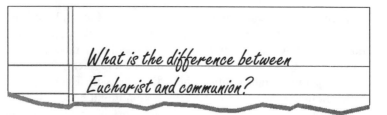

What is the difference between Eucharist and communion?

Eucharist is an activity. Communion is part of that activity. Eucharist is a two-fold celebration made up of the Liturgy of the Word and the Liturgy of the Eucharist. In that celebration we enter into the ongoing experience of Christ's passion, death, and resurrection. We say that we "remember" that experience, but it is deeper than just remembering. We actually become a part of that reality. In that way, Christ's presence becomes real for us.

In order for Christ's presence to become that real for us, several things will happen. There will be a gathering of believers. God's Word will be proclaimed. A eucharistic prayer, composed according to an ancient outline and proclaimed by an ordained presider, will be prayed over gifts of bread and wine. And the assembly will receive communion.

Communion by itself, without the celebration of the Eucharist, is a reminder of the eucharistic liturgy and is in a powerful way the presence of Christ. But it is not the full celebration of the gathered assembly. Receiving communion apart from Mass is helpful and sometimes necessary, but we never want to confuse that with the celebration of Eucharist, which is the core of our faith.

In what way is the Eucharist a sacrifice?

To understand the Eucharist as a sacrifice, it is important to understand something of what Jesus understood about sacrifice. That is to say, it is important to understand the Jewish practice of sacrifice. In Jesus' time, all Jewish sacrifice took place in the Temple in Jerusalem. There were three forms of Jewish sacrifice: whole, burnt offerings, which were a gift to God; sin offerings, which involved policies about the use of the blood from the sacrifice for the reparation of the sin; and peace offerings, which the worshiper was allowed to eat as a guest of the Lord.

The Passover sacrifice is an extension of the third type. Recalling the night the angel of death passed over the homes of the enslaved Israelites in Egypt, the paschal lamb was sacrificed every year in the spring at the Temple. The heads of households would take the lamb home to celebrate the seder meal with their families. After the destruction of the Temple in 70 CE, the Jewish community no longer had access to a sacrificial lamb because it could only come from the Temple. Very quickly the *matza* or unleavened bread began to take on the symbolism of the passover lamb.

Jesus had identified his body with the bread used at the Last Supper and with the passover lamb. The Gospel writers no doubt emphasized these associations especially considering the Jewish practice of connecting the sacrifice with the bread. These associations give us a rich system of symbol and metaphor for fathoming Jesus' sacrifice for us.

However, unlike the Passover lamb, which was sacrificed once a year, Jesus, the Paschal Lamb, died only once. In the Eucharist, when the bread and wine are broken and poured out, we are not re-sacrificing Jesus' body and blood; we are, instead, participating in the one sacrifice, which has already happened but which transcends time and place. Jesus' sacrifice is eternal and is present or actualized in every moment of history—past, present, and future. Our weekly memorial of that sacrifice allows us to be present to it, to make it real for ourselves. But more than that, our weekly Eucharist is a way for us to join ourselves with Jesus' sacrifice so that, just as he is offered, we are also offered.

In what way is the Eucharist a meal?

Again, it is important to understand what Jesus—and the Jewish tradition he came from—understood about meals. In the Gospels, every meal in which Jesus participated was a sacred and symbolic event. Meals are important.

Jesus ate with tax collectors and sinners. He ate with the multitudes when it first looked like there would not be enough for everyone. He often ate with his disciples and in doing so shared his life with them. These meals that Jesus shared in his ministry were the prefigurements of the Eucharist we share every Sunday.

Meals are important because they satisfy hunger and thirst. But eating a meal is more than just meeting basic nutritional needs. What makes a meal different from merely eating is the identification of our hunger and thirst with that of all humans who have ever hungered and thirsted. In our eating, we are thankful that we do not starve, and we are thoughtful of those who do. We are also mindful of the many human hungers that cannot be satisfied by eating and drinking. Our meals can be prayers that we will hunger and thirst only for what is right and good.

Drinking wine, in particular, can be a prayer for justice. Symbolically, wine liberates us from the constraints of this world. It affords us a new vision. We are infused with a new spirit. Our cares seem lighter and our hearts more joyful.

Wine also signifies the blood that is shed by the oppressed. By pouring out wine at the meal and sharing it, we share in the lives of all those who have suffered for their faith and have shed their blood for their beliefs.

Eating bread can also be a prayer of solidarity with the oppressed. The process of getting bread is symbolic of the birthing, living, dying, and re-birthing that take place in all our lives. It is symbolic of the crushing, pushing, burning, and brokenness that so many people suffer. A grain of wheat fights the elements for food, sun, and water. Having survived, it is cut down in its prime to bring profit to the harvester. It is stripped, crushed, and ground down. It is mixed, kneaded, and baked in an oven. It has become something new and nourishing, only to be broken apart again, chewed, and swallowed. Eating bread reminds us of all the life and death struggles of the lives that have worked to bring us our food.

The meal can also be an act of reconciliation. Meals always involve others. We share our food together as a sign of love and commitment. Even when we do not like those we eat with, we all try to get along for the sake of the "meal" and for the sake of the community. Meals are feasts and banquets. They are celebrations of the large and small events of our lives.

And meals are covenants. We seal our marriages with a meal. Successful contract negotiations often end in everyone going out to dinner together.

In addition, meals are memorials. In the meal we remember. We remember birthdays and anniversaries and the last Christmas grandpa ate at our table. We remember our salvation at Thanksgiving dinners and our liberation at Fourth of July picnics.

The Eucharist is a meal in all these senses. But it is perhaps the sense of meal as memorial that is most important. In the Eucharist, we remember Jesus. We do not merely recall what he did and the kind of person he was, although that is important. But the eucharistic meal we eat is a remembrance in the sense of "making present." When we "remember" our struggle for independence during our Fourth of July celebrations, we make present again what our forbearers believed about living as free people. In remembering, those ideals become present in us. We become one with the revolution. And in remembering year after year, we help the next generation to "remember" what it is to be an American.

When we "remember" the paschal mystery—Christ has died, Christ is risen, Christ will come again—every week in the Eucharist, we participate in the reality of Jesus. Jesus' presence becomes "real" for us. And in celebrating the memorial every week, Jesus becomes real for the next generation—and for the whole world.

In what way is the Eucharist a story?

The Eucharist is a story in several ways. We obviously tell stories in the Liturgy of the Word. The eucharistic prayer contains a succinct story of our faith. But most important, liturgy is a story in its ritual structure. All good stories have a beginning, a middle, and an end. In the liturgy, the Introductory Rites are the beginning.

In the Introductory Rites, we come together as a community. That is the first part of our story. God sees us as a community of people.

The middle of our story is two parts: a call and a response. In the Liturgy of the Word, God calls us as a community. God calls us to faith—faith in Christ, faith in the Gospel, faith in the mission of the

63

Lord. This is an important part of our story. We are not called as individuals so much as we are called as a community. And it is God's call—God's word—that forms us as community. We know that whenever God speaks, creation happens. God's word creates us as a people of faith. In faith, we are moved to respond. Our response is to gather around the table and share a meal. In faith, we respond to God's Word by sharing in the body and blood of Jesus. In that sharing, we become the body of Christ. We know that Christ is the fundamental sacrament, or story, of God. We become the sacrament, or story, of Christ. And we know that the story of Christ is one of solidarity with the marginalized and outcast of society.

Therefore the final part of the story is going out from the Eucharist to tell the story of Good News, salvation, and liberation to the world. At the end of Mass, we are sent out into the world to gather people together and tell them the story. In that way, the story never ends. The everlasting reign of God becomes the story for all time.

These are only a few of the ways of understanding Eucharist. The *Catechism of the Catholic Church* lists at least twenty images and titles for Eucharist. The rich symbolism of the Eucharist is inexhaustible.

Explain exposition of the Blessed Sacrament.

T he exposition of the Blessed Sacrament was first recorded at the very end of the fourteenth century. At least three factors led to its development.

The first was the popular eucharistic piety of the twelfth and thirteenth centuries. During this time people began to treat the eucharistic bread as an object to be worshiped instead of a meal to be shared. Around the year 1200, the bread and wine (but especially the bread) began to be elevated during the consecration. This moment soon came to be considered the high point of the Mass. Many people would leave the church after the elevation, some of them so they could hurry to the neighboring parish in time to witness the elevation at that Mass.

The second factor was the way the eucharistic bread was used to minister to the dying. Until this time, the dying were given *viaticum* or communion for the journey. But in the thirteenth century, the practice of merely showing the consecrated bread to the dying sprang up in many places.

The third factor was the development of the Corpus Christi festival, which did not originally include a procession with the Blessed Sacrament. But by the early fourteenth century the procession was an obligatory part of the feast day.

These somewhat liturgical forms of exposition soon led, in some places, to the continuous exposition of the sacrament in a monstrance. At first, these monstrances may have been thought of as modified tabernacles—places that reserved but allowed viewing of the consecrated bread. The final development along this line was the emergence of Benediction.

There are two important things to remember about exposition, both then and now. First, all forms of exposition derive in some way from the liturgy. Second, no form of exposition is meant as a substitute for the liturgy. Indeed, all eucharistic devotion is meant to lead people into a deeper participation in the liturgy.

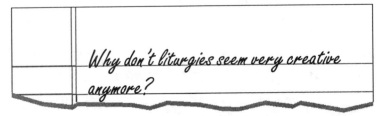

Why don't liturgies seem very creative anymore?

After several centuries of attempting to make the Mass strictly uniform in every time and place, the reform of the Second Vatican Council was like a breath of fresh air. Many communities began to take the mandate of the reform seriously and made sweeping changes in the way they celebrated liturgy. Some of these changes were good and others not so good.

In an attempt to save what is good and eliminate the not so good, most parishes are now trying to understand the traditions behind their symbols and rituals. The Council never intended change for the sake of change. Instead, the Council wanted the reformed liturgy to speak more clearly and honestly about our tradition of faith handed down from the apostles. Parishes are now asking what in our liturgies communicates our faith and what in our liturgies is simply clutter or extra words and symbols.

In the first few years after the reform, some liturgy planners sought to create meaning by incorporating symbols and ideas from the world around them. However, the elements of our secular world that we bring into the liturgy must also bear the weight of the mystery of our faith. So we have found through trial and error that felt banners, balloons, 1970s pop music, and most home-written prayers do not bear that weight.

Likewise, we are discovering that things in our secular world such as fire, bread, wine, water, oil, and touch *do* bear that mystery and do tell the story of our faith. Because these symbols are often the same ones that were so tremendously minimized in the pre-Vatican II church, we have trouble breaking old habits; we tend to keep these symbols small.

So we are in another transition moment. The "creative" things we did several years ago have lost their appeal, and we have not yet learned how to be creative with the symbols of our tradition. The solution is to recapture some of the enthusiasm we had for finding new things to add to the liturgy and apply that energy to maximizing the creative power of our traditional symbols.

Why aren't people doing plays and dramas as much in the liturgy anymore?

Communities have begun to question the reasons for wanting to do a play within the Mass. The answer usually has to do with making some part of the Mass, usually one of the readings or the Gospel, more relevant and interesting to the assembly. This perspective comes dangerously close to an understanding of the people in the pews as an "audience" that must be entertained by the "actors" in the play.

The Mass *is* a drama complete with a script, staging directions, props, actors, directors, and even an "audience." Doing a little play within the larger drama of the Mass disrupts the flow of the Mass and disturbs the relationships the Mass sets out to establish.

In the Mass, God is the audience, the priest and the other liturgical ministers are the directors, and the members of the assembly are the actors. Anything that casts the assembly in a passive mode takes them out of the role of actor and puts them into the role of audience.

The relationship of the actors to the script is also disturbed when a play is done. The script of the Mass is the dynamic relationship between Word and Eucharist that is played out through ritual storytelling and the use of meaningful symbols. When we insert another story with other symbols, the story of the Mass gets put on hold until we get finished with the new story. This interrupts and therefore weakens the connection of Word to the Eucharist.

What if the "new" story is an enactment of the Word? This *can* work but seldom does. First, which part of the Word is being enacted? Is it one of the first two readings? If so, how does that balance with the "script" of the Mass, which calls for the Gospel to be the most prominent of the three readings? If the Gospel is enacted, how does *that* balance with the "script" of the Mass which calls for the Gospel to be proclaimed by the pastor or leader of the community prayer? What if the presider is part of the little play? Does he wear a costume as the other members of the "play" do? If so, how does that balance with the ritual costume "scripted" for him in the Mass? If not, how does the smaller play qualify as an "enactment" of the Gospel? What if nobody is in costume? That can work, but the quality of the "actors" has to be high. Long pauses between lines, missed cues, and monotone reading will certainly be less proclamatory than having the presider proclaim the Gospel in a full voice filled with emotion. No chance of getting a reading like that from your presider? Well, it seems like that is the first task. Doing a play within the Mass on occasion will never counteract the problem of poorly proclaimed Scriptures. And if the presider and the other lectors become effective proclaimers, why would there ever be a need for a play?

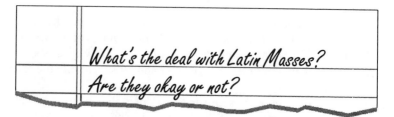

What's the deal with Latin Masses?
Are they okay or not?

There are several issues involved with Latin Masses. In the beginning, the language of the Mass was Greek. As Latin became more and more the common language of the people, the language of the Mass shifted to Latin also. This shift occurred gradually sometime between the third and sixth centuries. As time went on and languages changed, the Mass remained in Latin because Latin came to be considered a holy language or a language set apart from the "common" languages of the day. For a while this was not much of a problem because many people could understand some Latin, even if they could not speak it. But by the time of the Reformation, Latin was understood only by scholars and the clergy. The reformers found this untenable and demanded a change to the vernacular languages of the fifteenth century. The Council of Trent, to protect against the excesses of the Reformation, said the Mass *could* be in the vernacular but there was absolutely nothing wrong with Mass in Latin. And just to prove it, the Council of Trent decreed the language of the Mass must remain Latin.

Four hundred years later, the Second Vatican Council said that, as the church has always taught, there was nothing wrong with the vernacular, so the Mass could be celebrated in either Latin or the native language of the people celebrating. But, whether celebrated in Latin or English (or Spanish, or Polish, etc.), Catholics had to use the new structure and prayers of the reformed Mass that were promulgated by Pope Paul VI shortly after the council. They could no longer use the old Mass.

Then very recently Pope John Paul II granted permission to the bishops to allow within their dioceses the celebration of the *old* Mass (called the Tridentine Mass) that, by law, must always be celebrated in Latin. Bishops are not bound to give this permission, but they may. Some have and some haven't.

So a parish may on any Sunday without any special permission celebrate the *reformed* Mass in Latin. This is the same Mass we celebrate every week, only everything is prayed in Latin instead of English.

In the usual celebration of the Mass in the vernacular, some parts may be done in Latin to maintain a link with our centuries of tradition. For example, the acclamations of the Mass might all be chanted in Latin or the communion procession song might have a refrain in Latin.

Finally, it is never proper to use the Latin liturgy in any way that would be seen as a protest of the liturgical reform.

Is it better to provide Masses in different languages for various ethnic groups or to have bilingual and trilingual Masses?

The situation varies from parish to parish. However, for more recent immigrant groups, celebrating Mass in their native language is a way for them to worship in the vernacular—a major reform of the Second Vatican Council. This is true even if the group is fluent in English but English is their second language.

Parishes often celebrate multilingual liturgies in an attempt to be multicultural—another major reform of the Council. A few places even carry this to the extreme so that they will sing a song or two or proclaim some prayers in languages other than English when the vast majority of the parishioners speak English as their first language. This is not really multiculturalism.

When we talk of the liturgy being multicultural, what we mean is the core or the Roman Rite ought to be able to be transplanted to any culture. Within that culture, the rites take on the flavor and style of that culture. If a culture is homogeneous, this is not difficult to do. However, in many areas of the United States, several different cultures exist side by side.

Language is one way to identify a culture—but it is only one way. Language should not be isolated from the other aspects of the culture it comes from. That is not to say we cannot ever use songs and prayers in other languages, but it is important to do so carefully. Liturgies that reflect a white American culture in the way they are celebrated but have a little Spanish or Vietnamese language thrown in are not really multicultural.

Ideally, all cultures within a parish would be equally open to other cultures and feel equally secure about their own place in the parish. That may be the case in some parishes. However, in many parishes, recent immigrant groups feel their position in the parish is somewhat precarious. For example, it is not unusual to hear Hispanic or Asian parishioners, who may be in the majority in their particular parish, speak of the parish as though it belongs to someone else.

In these instances it may be more pastorally sound to provide Masses in the languages of the various groups of the parish, unifying the music roster and choice of prayers as much as possible. The short-term goal would be to give everyone in the parish a sense of being at "home." The long-term goal would be to unite the various cultures into a truly multicultural worship. That might happen fairly quickly at major celebrations in the parish. It might take a generation or two to make truly multicultural worship a reality at every Sunday Mass throughout the year.

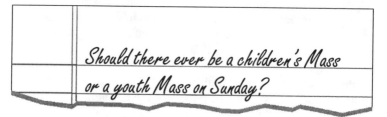

Should there ever be a children's Mass or a youth Mass on Sunday?

Some people argue that children and youth qualify as "ethnic" groups since their "cultures" are so different from adult cultures. Yet the goal of child-rearing is to successfully incorporate our children into the culture they were born into. Our goal would be to integrate children and youth into the regular Sunday experience just as we attempt to integrate them into the rest of our lives.

Many argue that children and youth feel regularly excluded from the primary Sunday Mass and that it is a matter of justice to provide an occasional liturgy "just for them." However, this is counter-productive to the purpose of the Mass. The Mass is supposed to welcome everyone. If our Masses are not doing that, not only are the children and youth being deprived, but so are the adults. The adults are not learning to act like Christ when he welcomed the little children. If we provide some separate time and place for the children to worship, not only do we deprive the children of their opportunity to evangelize the adult community, we also let the adult community off the hook.

Nevertheless, there are times when children and youth might worship as a separate group; however, these times would not be on Sundays or feast days (community days). These times would be during the school day, as part of the religious education program, as part of a retreat, and the like. In these kinds of liturgies, the particular needs of the children can be attended to without creating a sense of exclusion or isolation. However, even these non-Sunday Masses, like all Christian prayer outside the Sunday Mass, are still intended to flow from and lead back to the Sunday assembly.

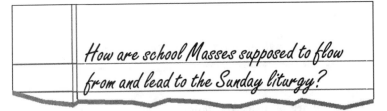

How are school Masses supposed to flow from and lead to the Sunday liturgy?

A generation ago, Catholic school children went to Mass every day. The music we sang was the same music we sang on Sunday. The prayers were the same. The ritual was the same. The only way one could really tell the difference between weekday Mass and Sunday was the first two thirds of the pews were filled with uniformed school children during the week.

Although that model is a bit extreme and seems outdated, the result was that after eight years of Catholic school, children could "do" the Mass from memory. It was in our bones.

The primary purpose of a *Catholic* school is to teach children how to "do" the Mass. If it is not the number one reason, it has to be in the top three. What is unique about a Catholic school? Many other private schools have small class sizes, good discipline, high moral standards, and many more of the fine features we can find in our Catholic schools. The thing they do not have is Catholic faith, Catholic prayer, and Catholic liturgy.

The thing that has always been true of Catholics is that our faith is most fully expressed, and therefore most fully known, at Sunday liturgy. The documents of the Second Vatican Council refer to the Sunday liturgy as the "summit and the source" of all our activity in the church.

This being the case, we could say the goal of every Catholic school would be to teach children to "do" the Mass. And the Mass children would know how to "do" would be the community Mass, the Sunday Mass. That does not mean school Masses must look exactly like Sunday Masses as they did in the past. It does mean that after six or eight years of Catholic school the children would know primary songs of the parish repertoire, they would know the basic prayers of the Mass by heart, and they would be able to identify the two primary parts of the Mass and have some basic understanding of how they relate to each other.

What role can children play in the liturgy?

The primary ministry for children, just as for adults, is that of being an active member of the assembly. Unfortunately, many of our worship spaces still have a "psychological communion rail." Everyone inside the imaginary line is considered to be actively participating, and everyone on the outside is considered to be somewhat more passive or inactive. The first task for a parish is to do liturgy in such a way that no member of the assembly, child or adult, feels any less involved or any less like a minister than any other member of the assembly.

Beyond that, children can serve in several specialized ministries at Mass. The most common choice is that of altar server. However, this is not necessarily the best place for children to serve. The altar server is supposed to be an assistant to the presider. The liturgy is a complicated ritual, and, to assist the presider as well as possible, the server needs to understand the structure and flow of the Mass. He or she needs to be able to anticipate problems and solve them. Very young children are incapable of this. Older children can usually handle the routine tasks without difficulty but are unable to deal with anything out of the ordinary. One solution some parishes have arrived at is to recruit *families* to serve at the altar. Adults in the family can handle complicated tasks, older children can do the routine things, and younger children can learn by helping and by example.

One job children seem very good at is hospitality ministry. Again, this can be a shared family ministry.

Although restricted by age in some dioceses, children also can be good communion ministers, especially in liturgies made up primarily of children, such as school Masses. Some people argue communion ministry is too important or holy to allow children to be involved in it. Oddly, the same argument is not made about children serving as lectors. However, when we look at the tasks children do, especially at home, many of them are helping to serve food at a very young age. Few if any are engaged in regular public speaking. In fact, it is the rare child who can serve as an effective lector (and that would include reading the intercessions). As children reach their teen years, they can more effectively serve as readers.

Children also can be involved in all aspects of the music ministry, according to their ability. And any time there is a procession in the liturgy, children can carry streamers, banners, incense, bells, or simply themselves.

> *Our school wants to use "On Eagle's Wings" as an entrance song for the eighth grade graduation Mass. Isn't that actually a funeral hymn?*

On Eagle's Wings" is a slightly adapted version of Psalm 91. The ancient tradition of the church is to use a psalm for processional moments in the Mass. In more recent times the processional psalms have been reduced to only refrains. You will still see that in missalettes. They are usually identified as "Entrance Antiphon" and

"Communion Antiphon." These antiphons are not read if songs are done in those places, which is usually the case.

It is appropriate to sing a psalm during processions. Psalm 91 may be used as an entrance song if the text and the mood of the song fit the occasion or the Sunday. However, it is important that the entrance song be a song the assembly knows and sings well.

There is no restriction that says Psalm 91 must be used only for funerals.

What are Mass stipends?

Mass stipends have a long and complicated history. They have their roots in the shift from the offering of bread and wine by the community to an offering of money both for the purchase of the bread and wine and for the support of the clergy. This became more common from the seventh century onward. By the eighth century, the connection between the offering of money and the presentation of the gifts for the Eucharist had completely broken down. By this time, donors were paying an honorarium to the presider before the liturgy with the expectation that the Mass in question would be celebrated only for the intention specified by the one who made the donation. It was not even required that the donor be at the liturgy. It was this stipend system that contributed to the rise of the "private Mass." To meet all the requests, more and more Masses had to be celebrated. In some periods of history in some regions, priests were ordained solely to celebrate these private, stipended Masses. As the Mass became more exclusive and the participation of the assembly more minimized and even eliminated, Mass stipends became one of the few ways in which lay people could have a role in the liturgy.

The Mass stipend system can easily become an abuse of the liturgy, and the Mass stipend system has undergone reform several times. Nevertheless, it is still practiced in the post-Vatican II church. An individual may make a donation and thereby obligate the priest to exclusively celebrate the liturgy for the intention of the donor. However, the donation is usually small, and priests no longer add Masses to their schedules simply to fulfill requests. In most Sunday bulletins, a list of the regular weekday Mass schedule is given and next to each Mass is the name of the donor who gave a stipend for that Mass or the name of the person for whom the Mass is intended. But even the sense of the Mass being celebrated for a single intention is diminished because of the presence of members of the community who are there praying for their own intentions and who have as much access to the grace of the Eucharist as does the presider. In fact, even the presider can have more than one intention although he can only take *one* stipend.

The stipend system is problematic and sometimes confusing. Ideally, those who want to pray for a particular intention can be invited to join the eucharistic community and offer their prayer as part of the celebration.

Ministers

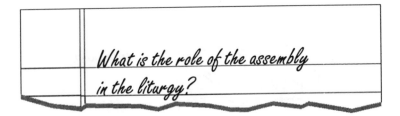

What is the role of the assembly
in the liturgy?

The shift in our understanding of the role of the assembly in the liturgy is one of the most dramatic changes brought about by the Second Vatican Council. The full implications of this shift are not yet fully realized. It is still difficult for those of us born before Vatican II to grasp the reality that we, as the liturgical assembly and as the body of Christ, make up the royal priesthood that offers the sacrificial memorial of the Eucharist.

The *General Instruction of the Roman Missal* puts it this way:

> In the celebration of Mass the faithful are a holy people, a people God made his own, a royal priesthood: they give thanks to the Father and offer the victim not only through the hands of the priest but also together with him and learn to offer themselves.

The magnitude of this priestly responsibility led the U.S. bishops to say in their document *Environment and Art in Catholic Worship*, "Among the symbols with which liturgy deals, none is more important than this assembly of believers....The most powerful experience of the sacred is found in the celebration and the persons celebrating, that is, it is found in the action of the assembly..." (28, 29).

The role of the assembly, then, is to *do* the liturgy. But *doing* the liturgy does not mean simply paying attention, singing the songs, responding to the prayers, and receiving communion. To do our job correctly, we celebrate the liturgy in such a way that it permeates our souls and changes our hearts. We then carry the liturgy in our hearts out into the world and continue *doing* the liturgy beyond the walls of the church. In that way, we sacrifice ourselves for the sake of the world. That is our role as a royal priesthood.

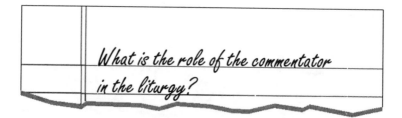

What is the role of the commentator in the liturgy?

Commentators were introduced into the liturgy after the Second Vatican Council to help people better understand the changes in the Mass. The *General Instruction of the Roman Missal* says: "The commentator gives explanations and directives to the people; he introduces the celebration and helps the people to understand it better. His comments should be carefully prepared, clear, and succinct."

As the "new" Mass becomes more and more familiar, the role of the commentator becomes less and less necessary. It is probably the case that by this point almost no Catholic needs to have any part of the Mass explained. The Mass should be familiar and understandable by now. This is true for anyone raised in the Church since Vatican II.

If your parish is using a commentator, it may be the case that the parish is trying something new. Perhaps at a baptism at Mass or at one of the rites of Christian initiation for adults, a brief announcement before Mass may be helpful. But usually, the role of the commentator seems less necessary than in the past.

The guiding principle is that whatever we do in liturgy be so clear as to require no explanation at all. This is, of course, not so in every parish. However, a parish would be better off putting its energy into making the symbols and rituals clearer rather than training a team of commentators to explain them.

In many parishes there already exists a group of dedicated folks who have been trained for this ministry and enjoy serving in this way. The question is what to do with them. Such parishes might not want to do away with the ministry altogether; they might gather all the commentators together for a meeting or a series of meetings to discuss the role of the commentator in the post-Vatican II era. The discussion might be about how the ministry has evolved and what the next phase of the evolution might be for them in their particular parish.

In some places, commentators might want to become lectors. Or they may decide they want to take charge of the announcement time. Or they may become a group of ministers whose sole ministry is to listen to the needs of the parish, translate those needs into intercessions, and proclaim the intercessions at Mass. Or they might become animators for the hospitality ministry. At any rate, it is a slow process, and it is a process the commentators would best be involved in helping to shape.

Is it all right to have more than one cantor at Mass?

The primary purpose of the cantor is to lead the assembly in song and to encourage the assembly to sing, to proclaim the Word of God in singing the responsorial psalm, and to assist with other responsorial singing. The number of people who do this ministry at a given liturgy is not important. In fact, *Music in Catholic Worship* says, "Provision would be made for at least one or two properly trained singers, especially where there is no possibility of setting up even a small choir" (35).

What is important is that the assembly is given clear direction and feel invited to participate. If two or three cantors seem to the assembly to be a small singing group that is focused on itself or is singing only to demonstrate its own virtuosity, the assembly is not likely to participate. If, however, two or three cantors join together to give strength to each other and out of that confidence they lend confidence to the assembly, they are acting as effective liturgical ministers.

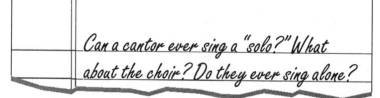

Can a cantor ever sing a "solo?" What about the choir? Do they ever sing alone?

Yes, especially during the verses of the responsorial psalm. Too often, however, the bulk of rehearsal time and energy is spent on these solo pieces. The result is less time given to practicing the music the assembly will sing and practicing ways of enhancing the music the assembly will sing.

Any liturgical minister functions only to serve the assembly and the liturgy. Given that, there would never be a time when the flow of the liturgy is interrupted to listen to a piece by the cantor or the choir. A common mistake, for example, is the "communion meditation song." There is no such song assigned in the Mass and to add one disrupts the crucial flow of the communion rite.

Music ministers will want to first ask what are the primary sung parts of the liturgy and work on these until they and the assembly can sing them almost by heart. Then, when those songs are mastered, the cantor and choir can move on to enhance the assembly's song with descants, harmonies, and interludes.

Finally, when that work is finished, the musicians might ask if there is any further way to enhance the liturgy with the addition of pieces that would be sung only by the cantor or choir.

Once the primary music of the assembly has been attended to, some places for choir anthems, cantor solos, or instrumental music include a prelude before the liturgy begins, music during the preparation of gifts, a recessional song (if a communal song of praise has concluded the communion rite), and a postlude.

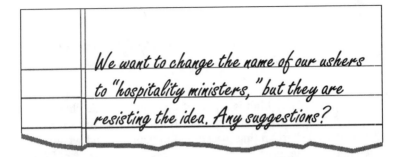

We want to change the name of our ushers to "hospitality ministers," but they are resisting the idea. Any suggestions?

Changing "ushers" to "hospitality ministers" may or may not be a good idea. One problem with having hospitality ministers, no matter what they are called, is that the members of the parish might come to think that hospitality has been taken care of and that they are relieved of the responsibility.

The central meaning of the paschal mystery is hospitality. The paschal mystery is the mystery of Jesus' sacrifice of himself for the sake of others. That is the same action we engage in when we are hospitable. We give up some of our own comfort so others will be comfortable. Guests get the best chair, the biggest slice, the first choice, and the last piece. We go out of our way to make the other person feel at home. That is a risk. We risk giving up something precious to us so the other person will feel comfortable. If we hoard that which is valuable to us, or we extend ourselves only a little, we are not really being hospitable. We are not being Christ-like.

So hospitality is about dying to ourselves. Every person in the parish is called to do that. Because there is a designated group standing at the door saying "hello" as people walk into church, that does not mean the rest of the community is relieved of the sacrifice of hospitality.

If the ushers and the parish understand that, it does not matter what the hospitality ministers are called.

Can blessings be given only by a priest?

A blessing of any kind is a part of the liturgy of the church. As with any liturgy, a blessing is a celebration in the priesthood of Christ. We all share in that priesthood in baptism, and we all can, when appropriate, give or celebrate a blessing. The *Book of Blessings* identifies a hierarchy of ministers who exercise the priesthood of Christ through the ministry of blessing. Article 18 says that at celebrations involving the entire diocesan community, the bishop is the minister of blessing. At celebrations which involve the community at which the bishop is not present, a priest ordinarily presides. And if a priest cannot be present, a deacon or layperson, by virtue of the priesthood of baptism, may preside over a blessing.

However there are some blessings, especially those associated with the family and the home, at which lay people are the most appropriate presiders.

Since a blessing is part of a liturgy, it needs to follow the requirements of good liturgy. The first of those requirements is the full, conscious, and active participation of the assembled faithful. Even if only a few of the faithful can be present, their presence strengthens the symbol of the church gathered in prayer.

A blessing typically has two parts: 1) the Word of God and 2) praise and petition. A blessing has a proclamation of Scripture because all creation and all we offer to God for blessing comes about because of God's creative Word. The second part, praise of God and petitioning for our needs, is the actual celebration of the blessing itself.

Signs of blessing often help to enrich the liturgy. These include the stretching out of the minister's hands, the laying on of hands, tracing the sign of the cross, sprinkling with holy water, and the use of incense. However, it is important to see these signs in the context of the entire liturgy of blessing. To isolate these signs as the only action of blessing is dangerous. The General Introduction to the official *Book of Blessings* reads:

> The outward signs of blessing, and particularly the sign of the
> cross, are in themselves forms of preaching the Gospel and of

expressing faith. But to ensure active participation in the celebration and to guard against any danger of superstition, it is ordinarily not permissible to impart the blessing of any article or place merely through a sign of blessing and without either the word of God or any sort of prayer being spoken (127).

Art &
Environment

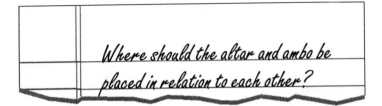

Where should the altar and ambo be placed in relation to each other?

The bishops' statement *Environment and Art in Catholic Worship* says,

> The location of the altar will be central in any eucharistic celebration, but this does not mean it must be spatially in the center or on a central axis. In fact, an off-center location may be a good solution in many cases. Focus and importance in any celebration move with the movement of the rite. Placement and elevation needs to take into account the necessity of visibility and audibility for all (73).

The document is silent on the actual placement of the ambo. However, the document does stress that all liturgical art is to be at the service of the liturgy to aid the action of the ritual.

The *General Instruction of the Roman Missal* states,

> The dignity of the word of God requires the church to have a place that is suitable for proclamation of the word and is a natural focal point for the people during the liturgy of the word....As a rule the lectern or ambo should be stationary, not simply a movable stand. In keeping with the structure of each church, it must be so placed that the ministers may be easily seen and heard by the faithful (272).

And the *Introduction to the Lectionary for Mass* reads,

> The Church has honored the word of God and the eucharistic mystery with the same reverence....The Church is nourished spiritually at the table of God's word and at the table of the eucharist: from the one it grows in wisdom and from the other in holiness (10).

If the ambo is to serve the action of the liturgy, it is important to place it in such a way as to give it some complementary relationship to the altar. It needs to be placed in such a way that any minister standing at the pulpit does not feel off to the side or back a little.

One current trend is to place the ambo to the side and several feet behind the altar. The reason often given for this is to provide better eye contact between the proclaimers and most people, especially if the seating is three sided. Oddly, this same argument is not made for the prayers and actions at the altar. Why is eye contact only important for the first half of the Mass?

It would be difficult to say a pulpit can *never* be placed to the side or to the back. However, wherever the ambo is placed, the emotional feeling of the minister at the ambo ought to be on a par with being at the altar. If, for example, the homilist feels a need to move out from the ambo to connect with the assembly, the ambo is misplaced.

How should the altar and ambo relate to the assembly?

We are all familiar with long churches in which the pews all face one direction and the altar and ambo are placed at the far end. This design dates from when the altar area was considered too holy for ordinary lay people. The priest would be "up there" with the altar boys, and that is where Jesus would become present. Those in the pews only needed to see the bread as it was lifted up during the moment of consecration.

Our understanding of Eucharist underwent a significant shift during this century. It became clearer to us that Christ was not present only "up there" but among all of us as well. It became clear that we are all called to gather around the altar to share in the sacred bread and wine, the heavenly banquet.

Some newer and renovated worship spaces reflect this new understanding of Eucharist. It is now possible to find spaces where the pews or chairs are arranged so they seem to enfold the altar. The space is arranged so the ambo relates to the assembly as a place of proclamation and prophetic teaching. This usually results in some members of the assembly being able to look directly across the room into the eyes of the Body of Christ—that is, their brothers and sisters in the assembly.

This is more than just a matter of turning the axis of pews to face a side wall. Many renovations have simply created a new way of establishing a "sacred space" and a separate assembly space. In many of these kinds of renovations, it would be an easy task to install a communion rail because it is so clear from the configuration of the furniture where it ought to go.

A worship space that seeks to embody the eucharistic theology of Vatican II is one in which the entire space seems sacred with no division between the altar, ambo, and assembly.

Why do vestments cost so much?

Vestments do not need to cost a lot. But they do need to be of high quality. We have lost a sense of how powerful vestments can be in celebrating the sacred mystery of the church. We are accustomed to putting our fine, ornamented, handstitched vestments from an earlier age in museums to look at on occasion. We would hardly think of creating such a vestment today.

But vestments, especially the vestments of the presider, are ritual garments that tell something of the story of who we are. Are we really a polyester community, held together with cheap thread? Do we really never need ironing, special care, or spot removal?

As the *Environment and Art in Catholic Worship* document states: "The color and form of the vestments and their difference from everyday clothing invite an appropriate attention and are part of the ritual experience essential to the festive character of a liturgical celebration" (93).

To have a vestment like that means making an investment. It may mean making an investment of money; it will certainly mean making an investment of time. It is important that the community shop for or design and create the best vestments it can to celebrate the liturgy as fully as possible. Procuring the right vestment is exactly like getting the right wedding dress (which is also a liturgical garment). Unlike the wedding dress, however, the parish vestments will serve the parish on many occasions for years to come.

The vestments usually belong to the parish. We need to move beyond thinking of the ritual garments as belonging only to the priest who wears them. Vestments that are bought or made by the parish usually remain in the parish for the life of the vestment. If the vestment is of high quality and is well cared for, that could be for at least a couple of our lifetimes. Even the most expensive vestments are not very expensive when the cost is spread over such a long period.

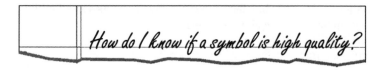

How do I know if a symbol is high quality?

The document *Environment and Art in Catholic Worship* says liturgy makes two demands on symbols: quality and appropriateness. *Quality*, says the document, is perceived only by contemplation.

To be able to contemplate symbols, they need to be large enough to be seen. Often the symbols in our liturgies are minimized to the point they are almost unnoticed. Symbols need to be large and full. Lots of water, lots of oil, lots of fire, lots of incense.

Symbols also need to be real. Contemplation reveals the honesty or dishonesty of a symbol. No artificial plant ever finally passes for a real one. Pressed hosts never make anyone think of real bread. Symbols need to speak for themselves. If they need to be explained, they are not working very well as symbols.

"Quality," says the document, "means love and care in the making of something, honesty and genuineness with any materials used, and the artist's special gifts in producing a harmonious whole, a well-crafted work" (20).

It helps to distinguish between primary and secondary symbols. Primary symbols are those that are most important in our liturgies. They are the symbols we cannot do without. They are the things that tell us of life and death. Liturgy planners need to focus on these primary symbols and make sure they are done well before anything else is done.

Some ways in which primary symbols are often minimized include the following. Only a trickle of water is used at baptisms. Likewise, confirmation includes only a thumb-print of oil. Not enough work goes into the proclamation of the Word. The bread used at Eucharist does not look or taste like bread. The cup is not shared with the assembly. Worship spaces have multiple crosses, minimizing the importance of the one cross of Christ.

Secondary symbols also need to be of high quality. Parishes will want to use good quality communionware and be sure that liturgical vestments are the highest quality the community can provide. Candles should be real. Avoid oil lamps and electric lights masquerading as candles. The communionware should also be of good quality. Take a look around your worship space and remove anything that is cheap, artificial, or flimsy.

Always remember, of all the symbols in the liturgy, none is more important than the gathered assembly.

The second demand on symbols is that they be *appropriate*. To be appropriate for the liturgy, a symbol must clearly serve the liturgical action. The primary aim of the liturgical action is the full, conscious, and active participation of the assembly in the ritual. Any artwork or symbol which enhances that participation is appropriate. Anything that minimizes that participation is inappropriate.

Imagine a Shakespearean play in which, during a scene change, one of the actors begins to sing an aria from a Wagnerian opera. Both are beautiful art forms, but it is inappropriate to mix the two. It is equally inappropriate to insert songs, poems, dramatic readings, dances, images, and other art forms into the liturgy that do not directly contribute to the action of the liturgy.

What defines good quality communionware?

Environment and Art in Catholic Worship says, "*Quality* is perceived only by contemplation, by standing back from things and really trying to *see* them, trying to let them speak to the beholder....Contemplation sees the hand stamp of the artist, the honesty and care that went into an object's making, the pleasing form and color and texture. Quality means love and care in the making of something, honesty and genuineness with any materials used..." (20).

The document specifically says about vessels that they "should be of such quality and design that they speak of the importance of the ritual action" (97).

We know this instinctively in our homes. We have the "good" dishes and the everyday dishes. The good dishes are of high quality and speak of the importance of the special meal in which they are used.

Communion vessels are thought of in a similar way. They might even be made of precious metals if the community can afford them. They also might be made of pottery, wood, or glass. But in any case they are to be made of materials that are considered nobel, solid, and prized. In no case would we want communion vessels to seem to be "everyday" dishes.

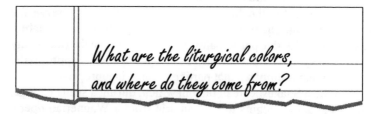

What are the liturgical colors, and where do they come from?

For more than one thousand years, no official colors were associated with the church year. Around the twelfth century, we get the first indication of a set correlation between particular colors and particular seasons. Surprisingly, that correlation was black for Christmas and Marian feasts and blue for Epiphany and Ascension.

Other color schemes began to develop, but the regulations governing the choice of color were local and customary. Different regions used different colors throughout the year. However, by the beginning of the thirteenth century, the Roman Rite had developed an official color scheme. White was used for feasts, red for martyrs' days, black for penitential days and seasons, and green for all other times. This was more of a guideline than a liturgical rubric until the Tridentine missal of Pius V in 1570. At that time the color sequence with which most of us are familiar was written into the liturgical books. However, regional differences still occurred in some places.

In current practice, the liturgical colors remain almost the same as before the Second Vatican Council. One significant difference is that white may now be used for funerals. Black, although seldom used, is still one of the options for use in the funeral rite (as is violet). Also, most parishes do not feel as restricted as before the Council to carry over the liturgical color into every facet of the environment. More of an effort is made to have the worship environment reflect or harmonize with the outdoor environment of the season.

Seasons

What is the liturgical year?

The liturgical year is the structure within which we celebrate the various aspects of the mystery of Christ's passion, death, and resurrection. The key to this structure is Sunday, the first day of the week, the day of the resurrection, and the day on which we regularly celebrate the paschal mystery.

Sunday is the original holy day. All other feasts and solemnities flow from our original celebration of Sunday. The first "holy day" to develop after Sunday was Easter. Easter was at first a two-day and then a three-day celebration which we now call the Triduum. The forty days of Lent soon developed as a preparation for the Triduum and a time of fasting and prayer for those who would be initiated into the church at the Easter Vigil. Lent begins with Ash Wednesday and ends on Holy Thursday.

The Pentecost season—the fifty days from Easter Sunday to Pentecost Sunday—also developed from the Triduum as a way to emphasize the importance of Easter and as a time of sacramental catechesis for the newly initiated.

Christmas is the other high point of the liturgical year, which, "next to the yearly celebration of the paschal mystery, the Church holds most sacred..." (*General Norms for the Liturgical Year and Calendar* 32). Christmas celebrates the incarnation of Christ. Christmas is not a day but a season that extends from the Christmas vigil on December 24 to the feast of the Baptism of the Lord in early January. Advent is the season of preparation for Christmas. It has the two-fold character of being a time to prepare for the memorial of Christ's first coming and a time to ready ourselves for Christ's second coming at the end of time. Advent consists of four Sundays, and the first Sunday of Advent is the beginning of the liturgical year.

The rest of the year is known as Ordinary Time. The word "ordinary," in this case, comes from the word "ordinal." You may remember ordinal numbers from grade school. The Sundays of this time are ordered by number and so they are "ordinary." But these Sundays are also ordinary in the sense spoken of before. It is Sunday that is the lynch pin for the liturgical year. In the seasons and holy days of the year, we celebrate different aspects of the life of Christ.

But in our ordinary Sunday celebrations, week after week, we celebrate what it is to be ordinary Christians. We are a people who mold our lives after the one who died, who rose, and who will come again.

What is the liturgical color for Advent?

The official color for Advent is violet. In recent years, some communities have begun to use blue for Advent to distinguish the season from the more penitential lenten period. Taking this trend into account, the Bishops' Committee on the Liturgy reiterated several years ago that the official color for the season remains violet.

However, there are shades of violet. A community might use deeper, bluer shades of violet for Advent, and warmer, redder shades of purple for Lent. Also note that the designation of liturgical color officially applies only to the vestment worn by the priest. A bluish-violet vestment might fit in well with blue and gray banners. Also note that no official color is designated for the candles on the Advent wreath.

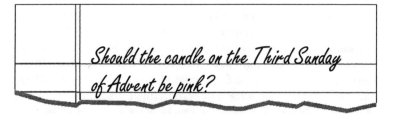

Should the candle on the Third Sunday of Advent be pink?

Pink or rose may be used as an official color twice in the liturgical year: the fourth Sunday of Lent (Laetare Sunday) and the third Sunday of Advent (Gaudete Sunday). The use of rose probably originated with the lenten Sunday in what used to be seen as a small moment of joy in an otherwise somber season. As Advent historically took on more of the penitential aspects of Lent in popular piety, it also took on its "Sunday of joy." *Gaudete* means "rejoice" and is the first word of the entrance antiphon for the day.

Again, this official color designation applies only to the vestment the priest wears. Interestingly, we almost never see a rose vestment in Lent and rarely see one in Advent. But the rose Advent candle often remains.

While there is nothing terribly wrong with this practice, it does call attention to an Advent piety that is no longer current. Advent was never meant to be a penitential season, and the reforms of the Second Vatican Council have helped us recall that. Using a rose candle on the Advent wreath in the midst of three violet or blue ones subtly gives the message that we might need a "Sunday of joy" in what is already supposed to be a joyful season.

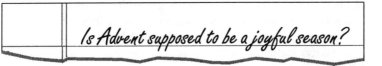

Is Advent supposed to be a joyful season?

Yes. It is a season of preparation for the coming of Jesus. It is a somewhat restrained time of year but still cheerful. It would be similar to preparing for a visit from a close friend or beloved family member. Lots of preparations need to be made, and our joy is not complete until the loved one arrives. But the preparation itself is also a happy time.

Since the Second Vatican Council, we have recalled the ancient meaning of Advent. Advent has a two-fold character. The first two Sundays focus on the coming of Christ at the end of time—the second coming. This emphasis flows naturally from the end-times theme of the last Sundays of the church year in November. The second half of the season focuses more on the incarnation of Christ as a child of Mary. Mary becomes a metaphor for us as church. Just as she received God-incarnate into herself, we are called to say "yes" to Christ's presence within us.

What are the O Antiphons?

The O Antiphons are now used as the alleluia verses in the weekday Masses in the week before Christmas. They originate from the Liturgy of the Hours, where they have been used as the antiphons for the Magnificat from December 17 to December 24. The composer is unknown.

The seven antiphons, when prayed in their original Latin, pray for the coming of the Messiah and begin with the word "O." Each antiphon names the Messiah using a different biblical motif. The antiphons have been recast into the classic Advent hymn "O Come, O Come Emmanuel."

The seven antiphons are:

1. Come, Wisdom of our God Most High *(O Sapientia)*.

2. Come, Leader of ancient Israel *(O Adonai)*.

3. Come, Flower of Jesse's stem *(O radix Jesse)*.

4. Come, Key of David *(O clavis David)*.

5. Come, Radiant Dawn *(O Oriens)*.

6. Come, King of all nations *(O Rex gentium)*.

7. Come, Emmanuel *(O Emmanuel)*.

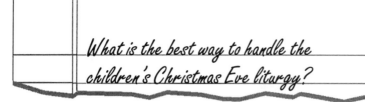

What is the best way to handle the children's Christmas Eve liturgy?

Christmas has become so commercialized and so centered on opening presents it is difficult to imagine we can ever rescue its original purpose. The proliferation of children's liturgies on Christmas Eve does not make the task any easier.

These are the reasons often given for having a children's liturgy on Christmas Eve: Christmas is for children; it is convenient for parents so they can spend Christmas with the children; it is the one time of year children really get to participate in a liturgy geared to them. Let's look at each of these.

Christmas is not just for children. In the United States, the secular markets have convinced us we have to buy many toys for the little ones to celebrate the Christmas spirit. But this is a recent development. Christmas is first and foremost a celebration of the incarnation of God. The story of God becoming human is a story of joy and wonder but also one of pain, suffering, and death. It is a story that is foreshadowed by and goes beyond the story of the baby in the manger. The celebration of the Feast of the Holy Innocents within the Christmas season gives us a clue this season is not just about candy canes and reindeer. Children need to learn this story, and they need to be taught what parts of the secular season can coexist with the spiritual season. However, Christmas can never be made exclusively or even primarily a children's holiday without losing the essence of our faith.

If the story of the incarnation of God is essential to our faith, then there can be no more important way of spending Christmas with the family than by celebrating that faith. The premier way that Christians celebrate their faith is in the liturgy. And so, Christmas Mass becomes the foremost family activity of the day. To focus the day on the opening of presents is to trivialize the tremendous and terrifying act of God becoming one of us.

Finally, if Christmas Eve is the only time of year children feel like a vital part of the celebrating assembly, all the more reason to immediately put a halt to a very destructive pattern. Children should not be restricted to a single day to be part of the community. It is best when children are a part of every Sunday Mass and holy day Mass in the parish. Whether on Sunday or on Christmas Eve, however, this does not mean we lower the standards of good liturgical prayer in a misguided attempt to entertain the children. That will not form them in the faith. Instead we use the fullness of the liturgical arts to engage the senses and the imagination of the children—and the adults—so they come to know God in the depths of their being. Having Santa show up at Christmas Eve Mass will not make that happen.

For parishes that do not have an early-evening Mass on Christmas Eve, it is probably best not to start one. For those that have one, it is best not to start a second one, as has happened in some places. Make all the Masses of Christmas Eve and Christmas Day full celebrations of song and spirit at which children feel equally welcomed and involved.

Where does the tradition of wearing ashes on Ash Wednesday come from?

In the early centuries of the church, people who had committed serious sin and wished to be forgiven would perform public penances. This sometimes included the penitents sprinkling ashes on their heads, which derived from the practice of public repentance in the Old Testament. By the Middle Ages, public penance had died out. However, in the tenth and eleventh centuries Christians began to take on a modified form of public penance at the beginning of the lenten season. They would come to church on the Wednesday before Lent to receive ashes. Men would be sprinkled over their heads with ashes and women would receive a cross of ashes on their foreheads. The ashes were made from the burnt palms from the previous Palm Sunday.

This ritual used to be done before Mass but is now done after the homily. A Mass is not required, however, and the ashes may be given in the context of a Liturgy of the Word.

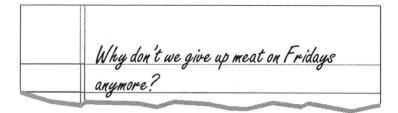

Why don't we give up meat on Fridays anymore?

Some Catholics still do. When the requirement to abstain from meat was lifted, it was done so Catholics might make their own choices about how to fast and abstain. But abstaining from meat was still recommended as a spiritual benefit. Then, in their statement on peace and justice, the U.S. bishops recommended that all American Catholics abstain from meat on Fridays as a reminder to work for lasting peace in the world and to pray for God's help.

Catholics are still required to abstain from meat on Ash Wednesday, the Fridays of Lent, and Good Friday. In addition, Catholics are strongly urged to abstain from meat on Holy Saturday as part of the paschal fast.

What is the Triduum?

The Triduum is a three-day celebration of the Lord's death and resurrection. It is the end of Lent and the beginning of Easter. The Triduum is the culmination and the high point of the church year.

The "days" of the Triduum are counted from the evening of Holy Thursday until the evening of Easter Sunday. This method of calculation has led to some confusion about which days are part of the Triduum. If we think of the new day as beginning with sundown—as the Jewish people do—the idea is easier to grasp. Sundown on Holy Thursday to sundown on Good Friday is one day, that is, Friday. The second day, Holy Saturday, begins with sundown on Friday and ends with the start of the Easter Vigil celebration. The Easter Vigil is properly thought of as a Sunday celebration, the third day, and not as part of Holy Saturday.

Several liturgies take place during the Triduum, but they are thought of as parts of one continuous celebration. The Triduum begins with the Mass of the Lord's Supper. The primary purpose of this liturgy is to commemorate Jesus' final meal with his disciples. This Mass has no formal ending; it just stops abruptly with no final blessing nor dismissal. This is because our celebration is not over. We gather the next afternoon for the reading of the passion and veneration of the cross.

Originally there was no liturgy on Good Friday. It was marked simply by the paschal fast (see page 110). By the fourth century, however, a liturgical commemoration of the day had begun to develop. The ritual was focused on the reading of the passion and followed by a veneration of the cross. It was not until the Middle Ages that communion from previously consecrated bread was added to the liturgy. However, at that time and until the twentieth century, the faithful usually did not receive communion, even at Sunday Mass. The Council of Trent in the later 1500s turned this custom into a prohibition against anyone other than the priest receiving communion on Good Friday. It was not until the reform of the Holy Week liturgies in 1955 that the faithful for the first time received communion on Good Friday. Some liturgists have called for further reform of this liturgy to return to the original celebration, which focused solely on the passion and the veneration, dropping the communion rite altogether. This would then create a true fast day in which we fast not only from food but from communion as well.

In most places, there is no liturgy on Holy Saturday. However, the Liturgy of the Hours is celebrated every day in monasteries around the world, and some parishes have begun to celebrate Morning Prayer and perhaps prayer in the afternoon on this day. This is also a day that has traditionally been reserved as a day of final preparation for the catechumens who are about to be baptized. Some rituals from the *Rite of Christian Initiation of Adults* also might be celebrated on Holy Saturday.

The Easter Vigil, St. Augustine said, is the mother of all vigils. It is the holiest of nights. It is the night when, as church, we are most true to who we are meant to be. If we celebrate no other liturgy all year, we should celebrate this vigil.

The Easter Vigil is a four-part liturgy divided into services of fire, word, water, and Eucharist. The Vigil *must* begin after dark, according to the rubrics of the liturgy. The new fire then breaks apart the darkness just as Christ breaks the darkness of sin that enfolds us.

In the Liturgy of the Word, we recount our salvation story. We tell the story for our own sake and for the sake of those present who will soon be initiated into our fellowship.

Having heard the saving call of God's word, the catechumens gather at the font of life and are immersed in the living water of Christ. And we renew our baptismal vows.

They then join us at the table, which is but a foretaste of the heavenly banquet we all await.

The Triduum ends with Evening Prayer on Easter Sunday. Most parishes do not actually celebrate this ritual. However, those parishes that do have found it a meaningful close to the three-day Triduum.

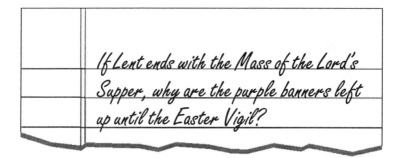

If Lent ends with the Mass of the Lord's Supper, why are the purple banners left up until the Easter Vigil?

They are not. The environment changes on Holy Thursday to an Easter environment. This does not mean a parish has to put out all the lilies for the Mass of the Lord's Supper, but the worship space should look more like Easter than like Lent. The rubrics call for the presider to wear a white vestment, and the liturgical environment is more harmonious when it does not conflict with his ritual garb.

Likewise, it is best if Good Friday is not a sea of blacks and reds. Some of these colors are fine, but you will still want the space to have an Easter feel to it. We do not celebrate Good Friday without the sure knowledge of the resurrection. We do not somehow pretend on Good Friday that we do not know about Easter. Good Friday *is* Easter.

The environment for these three days can be progressive. That is, Holy Thursday can be a foreshadowing of the full Easter glory. The several prayers of Good Friday (stations, seven last words, one or more celebrations of the passion) can each reflect a growing sense of Easter. If the church is open for prayer on Holy Saturday, still more of the Easter finery can be put in place. Finally, at the Easter Vigil, the full glory of the Easter season shines forth. Keep in mind, though, whatever is in place at the Easter Vigil is best maintained throughout all the Sundays of Easter. The fifty days of Easter are as one great day, one great Sunday.

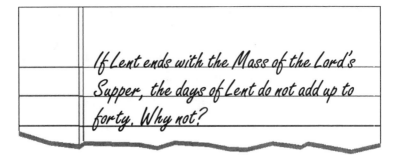

If Lent ends with the Mass of the Lord's Supper, the days of Lent do not add up to forty. Why not?

In the Roman Rite, Lent originally began on the sixth Sunday before Easter. That made for a forty-day season, which ended on Holy Thursday evening. However, Sundays were not considered fast days so Lent only had thirty-four fast days. In the fifth century, Good Friday and Holy Saturday became separated from the paschal Triduum and included in Lent. This increased the number of fast days to thirty-six. In the sixth century, Lent was beginning on the Wednesday before the sixth Sunday before Easter—what we now call Ash Wednesday—and Lent had its forty fast days. In the twentieth century, with the reform of Holy Week and the liturgical reforms of the Second Vatican Council, Good Friday and Holy Saturday were restored to their place in the Triduum. However, the church leaders did not think it would be pastorally wise to eliminate Ash Wednesday in order to begin Lent on the sixth Sunday before Easter. So in our current reckoning, Lent has thirty-eight days if you do not count the Sundays and forty-four days if you do.

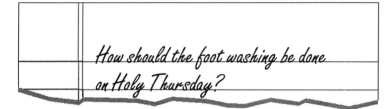

How should the foot washing be done on Holy Thursday?

The first question to ask is, "*Should* the foot washing be done?" The foot washing is a complicated ritual that, if not done well, is better not done at all. The rite is optional, and it is a fairly new part of the liturgy. It was not a part of the Mass of the Lord's Supper until the Holy Week reform of 1955. Foot washing does have an ancient tradition as part of some baptismal liturgies and some hospitality rites in religious communities, but its place in the Mass is an innovation.

If it is going to be done, it is important that all the elements of good ritual be in place. The symbols need to be large, the ritual needs to flow, the assembly must participate, and the liturgy should be better off for having had the ritual than not.

The primary action of foot washing is the washing of feet. This seems obvious, but some parishes have begun to wash hands or faces. And sometimes what takes place is not a true washing but a minimal wiping with a damp cloth. Bare feet are to be washed with at least as much water as you would use at home to wash your feet.

Keeping the ritual flowing while also significantly involving the assembly in the action can be difficult. The fewer people who actually get their feet washed, the smoother the ritual is likely to flow. However, if the number of people is too small, the assembly becomes a group of spectators. Not everyone has to get their feet wet to feel involved. But if the number is too small, the ritual can seem exclusive. There is no other point in the liturgy where any two people are interacting in such an intimate way for such a lengthy period. To open up that intimacy, the ritual must appear to be encompassing the entire assembly.

Some parishes have attempted to do this by moving the action out into the midst of the assembly—setting up washing stations in the aisles and at the ends of the pews. This can be effective depending again on the numbers and on the configuration of the worship space.

In the ritual, be clear that the presider is not the only person doing the washing and that those who are washed need not be only men nor need they number twelve. This is not the Last Supper. It is a commemoration of the Last Supper. We are not reenacting history, and we are not doing a play. Christ washed feet and told us to go and do the same. All of us are called to carry out the ministry of Christ in service to one another.

Also, the foot washing is not done as the Gospel is being read. The foot washing is not a dramatization of the Gospel. It is an independent ritual not to be layered onto another part of the liturgy. "Acting out" the foot washing during the reading of the Gospel puts too much of a literal spin on the Word and limits the symbolic power of the proclamation.

Finally, you will want to evaluate the foot washing every year close to the time in which it happened. Did it in fact enhance the liturgy? Would most of the assembly miss it if it were not done? Does it compete with the communion rite as a climactic moment in the Mass? How can it be improved for next year?

What is a paschal fast?

A paschal fast is the fast we make during the Triduum. It begins after the Mass of the Lord's Supper on Holy Thursday and is broken with the celebration of the Easter Vigil. The paschal fast is different from the penitential fast of Lent. During Lent, we are required to fast on Ash Wednesday and abstain from meat on the Fridays of Lent. To fast ritually means to eat only one full meal on a given day. We may eat two smaller meals if necessary for strength, but we may not snack between meals. During Lent, it is also customary to "give something up" like sweets or television. These fasts are penitential in nature. They are meant to remind us of our sin and strengthen us to live more Christ-like lives in the future.

The fast of the Triduum is entirely different in purpose. During the Triduum, we are required to fast on Good Friday, and we are encouraged to fast on Holy Saturday. Again, to fast means we eat only one full meal on these days. However, the paschal fast is not penitential. It is almost a joyful fast, a fast of anticipation. It is the kind of fast we experience when something big is about to happen and we are too excited to eat. The fast of the Triduum is also a more complete fast. Some people try to eat less food than they would during other fasts. Ideally, the paschal fast also means a fast from all activity that would distract us from preparing ourselves for the great celebration; it would be good to consider fasting from work, from television, from pleasure reading, from shopping, and from anything that takes our minds and bodies away from prayer and anticipation.

During our paschal fast, we want to keep in prayer all those who are preparing to enter the church through baptism at the coming Easter Vigil. These catechumens are also fasting and preparing at this time, and they are counting on us for our prayers and support.

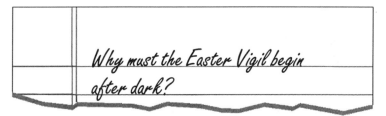

Why must the Easter Vigil begin after dark?

The power of any liturgy lies in the power of its symbols. The most important thing we say at the Easter Vigil is that Christ has broken through the sin and darkness of the world. Christ's light has shattered the darkness. In order to say that liturgically, there needs to be some darkness to shatter. And it needs to be very dark. True darkness does not occur until about forty-five minutes after sundown.

The image of Christ shattering the darkness also requires a light capable of shattering darkness. More and more parishes are beginning to use large bonfires for their paschal fire. When a fire of significant size is lit, it draws people closer. They come in out of the darkness and move toward the light. This movement is impossible if the assembly is sitting in pews and the paschal fire is lit in a small barbecue pit in the entry way of the church.

Finally, it is important that the paschal candle be of significant size. This light will lead the assembly through the Easter Vigil and through the fifty days of Easter. It will lead the catechumens to the waters of baptism. It ought to be a candle that can truly lead and not be dwarfed by the size of the worship space or the other liturgical elements.

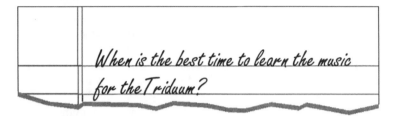

When is the best time to learn the music for the Triduum?

The Triduum is the crown of the liturgical year. Everything we do all year flows from and leads to the Triduum. If that is the case, we will be learning the music of the Triduum all year long. The music we sing at the Triduum will be the music we have been singing all year long. It is the music of our community that tells the story of who we are.

The music we sing at the Triduum needs to be music we can sing by heart, music we can sing in the dark, music we can sing while walking. We need to remember the music of the Triduum has to be music that has fed the catechumens all year and has led them to this great moment in our faith community. To do music on these days that is new or that is only done once a year will be difficult for the catechumens as well as for the community.

The best time to begin planning the music of the Triduum is as soon as possible after the previous Triduum. It is then that the music planner will know best what music worked and what music did not. Using the list of what worked well, add to it any songs the parish sings well that were not sung during the Triduum. If possible, use these favorites to fill the holes left by the "didn't work" songs that you remove from the Triduum plan. Now you have a master list from which to plan the music for the rest of the year.

Pay particular attention to music that will be used during the initiation rites for the coming year. Will the acclamations and songs of blessing be heard again during the Triduum?

Also pay attention to the psalmody used throughout the year. Will these same psalms be heard again during the Triduum, especially during the responses to the readings of the Easter Vigil?

If yours is a multilingual community, what work will be done during the Sundays of Ordinary Time to enable people of different tongues to sing each other's songs during the Triduum?

It may seem difficult, but stretch yourself to imagine ways in which even the music of Christmastide can find a place in the Triduum. Christmas is, after all, a feast that calls us to the paschal mystery. Ideally, there will be some musical bridge between Christmas and the Triduum.

One simple method for linking the music of the Triduum to other times of the year is to focus on a few basic hymn tunes. Most musicians know that all hymns have a tune-name. For instance, the name of the tune to which most of us sing "Praise God from Whom All Blessings Flow" is called OLD HUNDREDTH. Any text that has the same poetic meter as OLD HUNDREDTH can be sung to that tune. So OLD HUNDREDTH (or any other hymn tune your parish knows well) can be sung with several different texts for different seasons and feasts of the year.

There are many other creative ways to begin to link the music of the liturgical year to the Triduum. A short brainstorming session with yourself or other music planners will get you started. The key is to start as soon as possible after the last Triduum has ended. For those pieces of ritual music that are unique to the Triduum (e.g., Good Friday veneration), use the same pieces every year so they become a part of your local tradition.

Sacraments

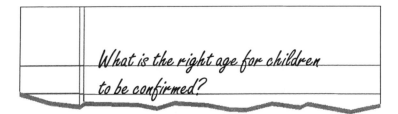

What is the right age for children to be confirmed?

That depends on what you understand the sacrament of confirmation to be. Most Catholics today were raised to think of confirmation as either a sacrament that made you a "soldier of Christ" or a sacrament that marked your entrance into "adult faith." Neither of these were the original theologies of the sacrament. The "soldier of Christ" image has a little more credibility, dating back to the Middle Ages. But the "adult faith" or maturity model is very new, dating from the middle of this century.

The reinstatement of the catechumenate has helped us recover the original theology of confirmation as an initiation sacrament. It is a sacrament of beginning. Adult catechumens are initiated in the same way the original catechumens were in the beginning centuries of the church. That is, they are baptized, confirmed, and receive first communion all in the same ceremony at the Easter Vigil. These three sacraments are celebrated in such a way that they seem as one. In fact, they used to be one.

In the early church, even infants were initiated in this way. However, in the fifth century, two things happened to cause the initiation sacraments to break apart. First, the church began to develop a theology of original sin, which soon led to infants being baptized as soon as possible after birth, no longer waiting for the Easter Vigil. Secondly, the church was growing at such a pace that bishops could no longer be at the baptisms of all these infants. To maintain some connection with initiation, the bishops required that they themselves be the ministers of confirmation. Originally, it was presumed that the family would take the infant to the bishop for confirmation as soon as possible after baptism. Eventually, because families more and more neglected to do this, the church had to legislate that baptized children be confirmed at least by the age of reason—or at about seven years of age.

In the late Middle Ages, the law evolved so that children could not be confirmed *before* the age of reason. That is our current law today.

Another factor in this development is that from the sixth century through the early twentieth century, there was a general decline in the reception of communion by the laity. If you ask some of your elderly relatives or friends, they will remember when Catholics only went to communion once a year—the Easter duty.

As a result, communion began to be seen as something too important and too special for a seven-year-old to understand. Communion began to be delayed later and later because the child was not considered mature enough to receive the sacrament. So from the seventeenth century until early in the twentieth century, a typical initiation process would be for a child to be baptized as an infant, be confirmed in early grade school years, and receive first communion in early adolescence.

Then a very important thing happened. In 1910, Pope Pius X wanted to encourage Catholics to share in communion regularly—daily if possible, but at least weekly at the Sunday Mass. One of the ways he did this was to remove the "maturity" aura from communion by lowering the age of first communion to the age of reason, or about age seven. Before this, confirmation was usually celebrated before first communion. But the logistical problem still existed that a bishop could not always get to a parish to celebrate confirmation in time for a child to be confirmed at age seven. So very often confirmation was delayed until after first communion. When that happened, it did not take long for confirmation to take on many of the "maturity" qualities that were no longer being associated with first communion.

The difficulty with this thinking is that spiritual maturity is not the same as psychological maturity. A seven-year-old can and sometimes does have more faith than an adult.

What is the right age for someone to be considered mature? In this century it has continued to float upward. In the 1970s, many parishes were confirming children of junior high school age. That began to move up to early high school. Now many parishes seem to be moving up to sixteen or seventeen as the designated age. Often the arguments for these delays have nothing to do with the theology of the sacrament but are instead focused on rationales for keeping teenagers in the religious education program.

The larger problem here is not what delaying confirmation does to the theology of confirmation but what it does to the theology of Eucharist. Eucharist is our most fundamental, most important sacrament. It is the font and source of all we believe as Christians.

When we say a child can receive Eucharist but is not yet "ready" for confirmation, we are holding up confirmation as a sacrament that demands something more. This is contrary to the teaching of the church and to our faith. So what is the right age for confirmation? Whatever we consider to be the right age for first communion. The rites themselves and canon law demand nothing more for confirmation than is required for the celebration of first communion. Some parishes and some dioceses are moving in this direction. Confirmation is being restored to its original place before first communion. In places where this is happening, confirmation is usually celebrated in conjunction with first communion when the candidates are around the age of seven.

If confirmation and Eucharist are both initiation sacraments, why not celebrate them together with baptism at infancy?

Initiation was celebrated this way in Rome until the twelfth century. It is still done that way in the eastern rite churches. However, to celebrate initiation this way in the Roman Catholic Church would require a change in canon law. Children may not be confirmed or receive first communion until they have reached the age of reason, or about age seven. This is a law that can be changed, but the church moves slowly. It is not likely to change anytime soon.

The more important issue is the question of sequence. Confirmation needs to be celebrated in such a way that it leads to Eucharist. And, if Eucharist is to be the culmination of our initiation, it is important to celebrate it in a way that emphasizes its climactic nature.

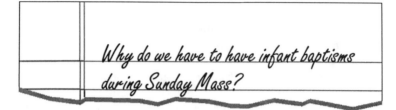

Why do we have to have infant baptisms during Sunday Mass?

We don't. However, Sunday is a premier time for baptism because it is the day of the Lord and the day of resurrection. Baptism is an important event for the parish. The goal would be that every parishioner be deeply concerned about the process of children entering the faith. Given all that, however, Sunday Mass is sometimes not the best time for infant baptisms.

First, the baptismal rite is often abbreviated so Mass will not run too long. Sometimes, parts of the Mass are also abbreviated, such as the homily or the music, to speed things up. These compromises often do nothing enhance the quality of the celebration.

Second, when an infant is baptized at Mass, it highlights the anomaly that everyone at the liturgy *except* the newly initiated is welcome at the table to join in Eucharist.

The argument for having baptism at Mass is that it is a community event and not a private affair. It is to be celebrated in the midst of the community.

The solution is somewhat simple. Baptisms can be scheduled on Sunday afternoons several times a year. The number of times per year can be calculated so an average of ten to fifteen babies are initiated at each baptism. When parents, godparents, siblings, relatives, friends, and neighbors all gather, the size of the assembly is large enough to be representative of the parish community. The liturgy would follow all the norms of good liturgy: full use of symbols, good music, skillful presiding (in full vesture), and dynamic preaching. In this way infants are clearly baptized into a *community* of faith, and they are baptized on the day of resurrection. The liturgy can be celebrated to its fullest without having to make compromises for the sake of time and efficiency.

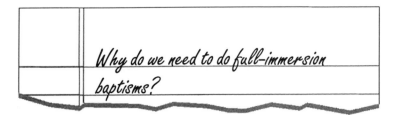

Why do we need to do full-immersion baptisms?

If you have ever witnessed a full-immersion baptism of either an infant or an adult, you will never want to see baptism done any other way.

The power of the symbol is so strong and so moving that, when baptism is done by full immersion, people's lives are changed. When new initiates go down into the water three times—in the name of the Father, in the name of the Son, in the name of the Holy Spirit—they die to themselves. They die to their old way of life. Even infants can be said to have died to the world and raised up again to a new life. All the imagery of washing becomes immediately clear; it does not need to be explained.

Some critics have said full-immersion baptism is not Catholic. That is not true. The *Rite of Christian Initiation of Adults* recommends full-immersion baptism as the ideal way to initiate. The practice dates from the baptism of Jesus in the Jordan.

In some churches it can be difficult to create a font large enough to immerse adults. However, many publications are giving parishes how-to articles on building temporary fonts (see the March 1995 issue of *Modern Liturgy* [22:2]). For infants, it is not too difficult to find a bowl or tub large enough to immerse them.

If you want to get your feet wet before diving into full-immersion, call around to find a parish that has done it. Interview them about their experience and plan to go to one of their baptisms. You will come away a different person.

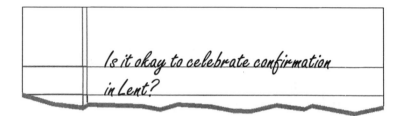

Is it okay to celebrate confirmation in Lent?

This question comes up more and more because of the restoration of the catechumenate. Parishes put much effort into helping the catechumens understand Lent as a time of preparation for the initiation sacraments, which will be celebrated at the Easter Vigil. Then, right in the middle of their preparation, the parish celebrates a big initiation moment with the teenagers of the community. The bishop comes, the church is full, there is much planning and partying. All this seems contradictory to what the catechumens have been learning about Lent as an ascetical season of fasting and preparation.

The practical reason some parishes celebrate confirmation in Lent is that confirmation preparation programs are often run on a school-year model. Children begin their preparation in September and have completed their preparation in the spring. The culmination of their preparation is focused on celebrating confirmation near the date of the completion of that preparation. For some parishes in the diocese, it works out that they are able to have this celebration in the Easter season or the early summer. The bishops of most dioceses, however, cannot get to every parish in the diocese in that time frame. Given the choice of delaying confirmation into the later summer months or celebrating the sacrament in the earlier spring, most parishes choose to celebrate confirmation in Lent.

However, as more parishes are experiencing the dissonance this practice causes with their catechumenate initiation process, they are choosing to delay confirmation until the fall of the following year. In a few dioceses, bishops are authorizing pastors or other desig-nated priests to serve as ministers of confirmation so more parishes can celebrate the sacrament in the Easter season.

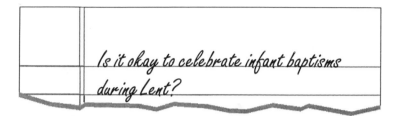

Is it okay to celebrate infant baptisms during Lent?

The only justifiable reason—if there is one—for celebrating confirmation during Lent is the schedule of the bishop demands it. That is not so with baptisms. Parish priests and deacons have the flexibility to arrange their schedules so that baptisms can be celebrated in the Easter season and other seasons outside Lent.

It may be idealistic to hope for, but, at least in smaller parishes, it is not unthinkable to schedule almost all baptisms—infant, child, or adult—for the Easter Vigil. The Vigil is *the* premier time for baptism, and families may begin to long to have their babies baptized at that great feast. Even in large parishes, the usual "Lenten" baptisms might be celebrated at the Easter Vigil and the bulk of the infant baptisms celebrated throughout the year.

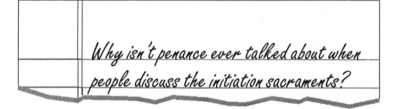

Why isn't penance ever talked about when people discuss the initiation sacraments?

Penance is not one the three initiation sacraments. In its origins, initiation was one event that included actions that later became identified by the church as distinct sacraments. These were baptism, confirmation, and Eucharist. Baptism has always been seen as the primary sacrament that forgives sins and reconciles us to God. In the early church, penance, or reconciliation, was treated as a "second baptism" that one could receive only once in a lifetime. It was a second chance extended to those who somehow didn't live up to the commitments made in their first baptism.

For historical reasons, the unity of the actions of initiation began to break apart. For one thing, due to the rapid growth of the church in the early Middle Ages, bishops were unable to preside at the initiation of every new Christian. Priests were delegated to preside. In the western church, however, bishops retained to themselves the right to preside over confirmation. At first, confirmation was delayed for only a few months to a year after baptism. Eventually, it came to be delayed for several years until the child had reached at least the age of reason (about seven years). First communion was delayed even longer until the child was "mature" (usually early puberty).

Meantime, penance came to be seen as a sacrament to be practiced regularly and not just once in a lifetime. However, it was never considered an initiation sacrament.

In modern times, the age for first communion was lowered and the age for confirmation raised. This further disintegrated the initiation sacraments by placing the final two out of order. Also, children began to be introduced to the sacrament of penance *before* they had made their first communion. Penance was originally a sacrament that restored one to communion. Now we have a practice in which some children who are not yet communicants are being "restored to communion."

The *Rite of Christian Initiation of Adults* is the latest church document on initiation. It restores the traditional practice of celebrating baptism, confirmation, and Eucharist in a single ceremony for anyone who has reached the age of reason without having been baptized. We can hope that further reform will restore at least the order of the initiation sacraments if not the unified celebration of them for the entire church.

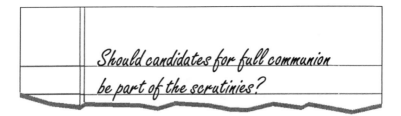

Should candidates for full communion be part of the scrutinies?

It helps to understand the purpose of the scrutinies. The scrutinies are meant to "uncover, then heal all that is weak, defective, or sinful in the hearts of the elect" (*Rite of Christian Initiation of Adults* 141).

That sounds like good medicine not only for the elect but for the candidates for full communion and the members of the Catholic faithful as well. Why not scrutinize everybody?

We do not scrutinize everybody because, as the rite goes on to explain, the reason for this healing of sin is for a specific purpose. It is to "complete the conversion of the elect" (RCIA 141) and to make the elect progressively aware "of sin and their desire for salvation."

The key point here is that the scrutinies are the final steps on the path of conversion, which leads to salvation.

Aren't we all in need of conversion and salvation? Yes and no. We all need to deepen and continue our conversion to Christ. But some of us can already claim to have been saved by Christ through baptism. We have crossed an important threshold in our conversion journey.

Candidates for full communion have already crossed that threshold also. They have been baptized and therefore saved. They may not believe it, they may not live it, they may not want it, but there it is. Nothing can change it. The proper place for them to *reclaim* their baptismal commitment and to ritualize a change of heart and conversion to a Gospel lifestyle is the same place members of the Catholic faithful reclaim their baptismal commitment—the sacrament of penance. Although many pastoral leaders will advocate including the already baptized candidates along with the elect in the scrutinies, the rite provides no such option. A ritual labeled "Penitential Rite (Scrutiny)" is provided for the candidates for full communion on the Second Sunday of Lent. The reason given for the separate penitential rite is:

Because the prayer of exorcism in the three scrutinies for catechumens who have received the Church's election properly belongs to the elect and uses many images referring to their approaching baptism, those scrutinies of the elect and this penitential rite for those preparing for confirmation and eucharist have been kept separate and distinct. Thus, no combined rite has been included... (RCIA 463).

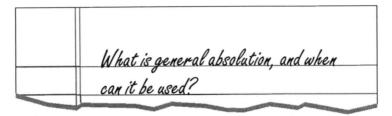

What is general absolution, and when can it be used?

General absolution is the ritual form of sacramental forgiveness given in the third form of the sacrament of penance. To understand it requires understanding the three forms of penance and something about the history of penance.

In the early church, people who had committed serious sin were thought to have abandoned their baptism. Some early church leaders talked about it as though one had fallen overboard from the ship of the church. Penance and reconciliation were talked of as a plank or life preserver thrown to the drowning sinner. But it was seen as a once-in-a-lifetime event—a kind of second baptism. Sinners entered an Order of Penitents and went through a process similar to the catechumenate in which they were dismissed from the Sunday assembly after the homily. Penitents had to pray, fast, and do works of charity. Penitents could not eat meat during the time of penance (usually several years), could not serve in the military, could not engage in trade, and could not bring a case before civil court. Penitents had to abstain from marital intercourse. Sometimes, penitents had to remain celibate for the rest of their lives. The entire process—like the catechumenate—was very public. The public nature of the process was intended as a strengthening for the penitents, not a humiliation. The church could witness the faith of the penitents and pray for them in a sign of solidarity.

In the ninth century private penance was introduced into the church by the monks of Ireland and northern Europe. Originally seen as an outgrowth of spiritual direction, this new form of penance lacked public rituals or acknowledgments. It was a matter dealt with between the penitents and the confessors. The bishops resisted this radically new form of penance, but parish pastors found it much more useful in meeting the needs of their parishioners. Eventually, public penance was required only for the gravest of sins and then not at all.

In an effort to combine the best of both systems, the Second Vatican Council called for a revision in the Rite of Penance. While private confession had met a great pastoral need, the communal nature of sin and reconciliation had been submerged. In 1973 the Congregation for Worship issued the new Rite of Penance. In that rite, three forms of reconciliation are given. Each form, however, has all the essential elements of sacramental penance, which are contrition, confession, penance (satisfaction), and absolution. Each form, even private confession, is a liturgy and therefore a "public" ritual of the church. The first form is individual confession and absolution, which is what most of us grew up with. What is different now is the emphasis on this form as a liturgy. Therefore, Scripture is always to be read and the liturgical gesture of laying on of hands is to be used. People may still go to confession anonymously but the ideal is a face-to-face encounter with the presider.

The *third* form is a gathering of an assembly of people. A full Liturgy of the Word is celebrated, including a homily. There is a general confession of sin—for example, praying the Confiteor—and the climax of the liturgy is a general absolution. There is currently a misconception that this form of reconciliation is illegal to use. It cannot be illegal because it is part of the official rites of the church. Its use, however, is more restricted. The restrictions vary from diocese to diocese. However, the general rule is that a parish is not supposed to *plan* for a celebration that would include general absolution. If, however, the number of penitents is so great that many would be unable to receive absolution from individual confessors, the presider may decide on the spot to issue a general absolution, according to diocesan norms.

The *second* form is a combination of these other two forms. There is a gathering of the assembly and a full Liturgy of the Word. Then, after the homily, penitents approach individual confessors for private confession and absolution. As the number of priests continues to decline, this form of the rite is becoming more difficult to carry out.

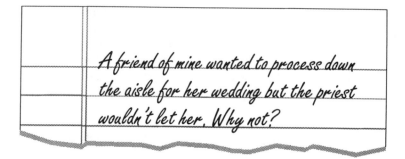

A friend of mine wanted to process down the aisle for her wedding but the priest wouldn't let her. Why not?

It was not that he would not let her process. It was that he would not let her process by herself or only with her father.

The practice of the father processing his daughter to the waiting arms of the groom dates from the time when women were dependent upon the men of the house for their identity. The symbolism behind giving away the bride is that she is moving from her father's house to her husband's. It is not a very good way to start a Catholic marriage, in which husband and wife are seen as equal partners.

Another thing to consider is what the solo procession of the bride does to the liturgy. The Introductory Rites in a Catholic liturgy are intended to call us together as a worshiping assembly. The actions of the Introductory Rites are intended to put the focus on the assembly. There may be a procession, but it ought to be a procession of all the ministers for the liturgy or at least the primary ministers. At a wedding, the primary ministers are the lectors, the presider, the bride, *and* the groom.

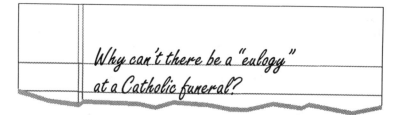

Why can't there be a "eulogy" at a Catholic funeral?

As with any public prayer for Catholics, the focus of the prayer is on Christ. A eulogy, on the other hand, focuses on the virtues of the deceased. Our single hope in the struggle against sin and death is with Christ and not with our own human virtue. A true homily helps the grieving community better grasp how the death of a Christian relates to the saving grace of the paschal mystery. The Christian funeral is the one place where the full cycle of the journey we began at baptism can be tangibly preached about. In baptism, we promised to die with Christ that we might also live with him. It would be a shame to abandon this moment to a biographical listing of the deceased's accomplishments in his or her life.

> *Does that mean nothing can be said about the person for whom the funeral is being celebrated?*

No, it is a matter of focus. The focus of the homily is on "God's compassionate love and on the paschal mystery of the Lord as proclaimed in the Scripture readings" (*Order of Christian Funerals* [OCF] 141). As long as that focus is maintained, some concrete references to the deceased is acceptable and appropriate. At the Final Commendation—which takes place following the prayer after communion—the focus of the rite is "a final farewell by the members of the community, an act of respect for one of their members whom they entrust to the tender and merciful embrace of God" (OCF 146). For that reason, the rite says at this point, "A member or a friend of the family may speak in remembrance of the deceased before the final commendation begins" (OCF 197). Still, this is not a eulogy in the traditional sense. From its placement in the rite, toward the end of the liturgy, this remembrance is best when prepared beforehand and brief.

Although not part of the official rite, it would make more sense to have an extended remembering or storytelling about the deceased at the vigil the night before. In this way, many friends and relatives could share at length about the gifts of their departed loved one. This extended storytelling would also help those who did not know the deceased as well come to know him or her better before beginning the funeral celebrations. Finally, though oftentimes hard to bear, families members can be consoled by hearing from those gathered how the deceased was thought of by others in the community.

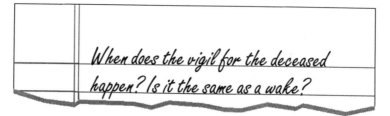

When does the vigil for the deceased happen? Is it the same as a wake?

There are three primary rites in the Order of Christian Funerals: the vigil, the funeral, and the burial or committal. The vigil is what we sometimes think of as the wake. The vigil usually takes place the night before the funeral, and it can take place in the funeral home or the church. Frequently communities are finding a vigil in the church to be a more comfortable and familiar setting than a funeral home.

The vigil can take one of two forms. It can be a Liturgy of the Word or a Liturgy of the Hours. The Liturgy of the Word is more common probably because people are more familiar with it. It is exactly like the first half of the Mass.

The Liturgy of the Hours, though less common, is an ancient and beautiful service. The Liturgy of the Hours is the celebration of either Morning Prayer or Evening Prayer (depending upon the "hour" it is celebrated). These prayers are composed first of praise and second of petitionary prayer. During the first half of the prayer, two psalms and a canticle are usually sung. This is followed by a short Scripture reading and a Gospel canticle. The second half of the prayer is intercessions, the Lord's Prayer, concluding prayer, and dismissal.

Since this liturgy involves quite a bit of singing, it is a good idea to have one of the parish musicians assist with the liturgy. The presider of the liturgy is often a priest, but it also may be a layperson.

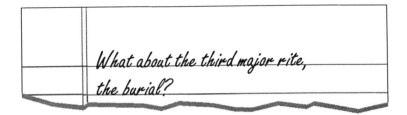

What about the third major rite, the burial?

The burial, or Rite of Committal, is the place where our Christian faith comes most into conflict with the efficient, death-denying conventions of the culture. Secular burials are quick, sanitized events that do their best to minimize the fact that a body is being buried (or burned or submerged at sea). In a usual burial, the body is carried a short distance from the hearse to an electric cart, which wheels it to the graveside. At the graveside, any trace of dirt is covered over with green carpet. Usually, after a brief service, the community is dismissed by the funeral director, and the body is only lowered into the ground after all have left.

A fuller, more Christian burial would have the body carried by pall bearers and led by a processional cross to the graveside while the community sings the litany of saints or a psalm. Once all were in place, the presider would invite the community to silent prayer. A brief Scripture verse would precede a prayer of blessing over the casket and the grave. This would be followed by intercessions, the Lord's Prayer, a concluding prayer, and a final blessing of the community.

Then, as the community sang songs they knew by heart (e.g., "Amazing Grace," "On Eagle's Wings," "Soon and Very Soon"), the body would be lowered into the grave. The community would continue to sing for as long as they felt moved to do so. Some would begin to leave, saying goodbye by throwing flowers or a handful of dirt into the grave. Others might bless the grave with holy water. Meantime, the cross-bearer would remain at the head of the grave until the last family member had left. The family would leave the graveside with the image of their loved one resting in the shadow of the cross.

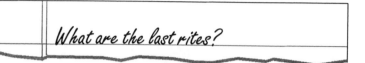

What are the last rites?

"Last rites" is a popular term used to refer to the anointing of the sick. But the anointing of the sick is not the "last rite" a person receives, and one does not need to be dying to be anointed. Anyone who is "dangerously ill due to sickness or old age" may be anointed, according to the introduction to the Rite of Anointing. The sick person is not to be anointed a second time unless he or she recovers and then falls ill again or unless the danger or seriousness of the present illness becomes more grave. A sick person would be anointed before surgery "whenever a dangerous illness is the reason for the surgery." Elderly people may be anointed if they are in a weakened condition even if no dangerous illness is present. Children may be anointed if they are old enough to understand the anointing and are able to take comfort from it. Generally, if they are old enough to receive communion, they are old enough to be anointed. An unconscious person may be anointed if it is clear the person would have asked to be anointed if conscious. However, a dead person is never to be anointed. A priest is the only minister who may anoint sacramentally. Deacons and unordained hospital chaplains are not given permission to minister this sacrament.

Some parishes schedule regular anointing or "healing" Masses in which sick people are encouraged to come forward for anointing. This has the advantage of making the community aware that the anointing is not reserved only to the dying. The disadvantage is it can lead some people to believe anointing is available for any illness, even if it is not a dangerous one.

Once someone has been anointed for an illness and that illness has progressed to the point of near-death, the proper "last rite" is *viaticum*, which is a brief communion service that takes place shortly before death. Communion is thought of as food for the journey the Christian is about to begin.

Call for Questions

Do you have a question that isn't answered in this book? Send it to me, and I'll make it part of a follow-up volume of more liturgical questions and answers. You can reach me at:

Questions
MODERN LITURGY
160 E. Virginia Street #290
San Jose, CA 95112-5876
Fax: 1-408-287-8748
e-mail: MdrnLitrgy@aol.com

Annotated Bibliography

Official Rites, Books, and Documents

The Constitution on the Sacred Liturgy. In *The Documents of Vatican II*, edited by Walter M. Abbot, SJ. New York: Guild Press, 1963. The CSL is the foundation of the entire liturgical reform. It is really not possible to understand much about contemporary liturgy without a close familiarity with this document. It was the first document produced by the Second Vatican Council, and it distills an international, one hundred-year liturgical reform movement. The most important principle in the document and in the liturgical reform is the full, conscious, and active participation of the assembly in the liturgy (14). So important is this principle, the CSL says, "in the reform and promotion of the liturgy, this full and active participation by all the people is the aim to be considered before all else. For it is the primary and indispensable source from which the faithful are to derive the true Christian spirit...." This document is sometimes referred to by the abbreviation SC from its Latin name, *Sacrosanctum Concilium.*

Sacramentary. New York: Catholic Book Publishing Co., 1985. The full version of the sacramentary was first published in 1970. It has undergone several minor revisions since then. A major revision of the sacramentary is currently in process for English-speaking countries. Depending upon the speed of individual bishops conferences in approving the changes and the rapidity of approval by Rome, the changes could become official in a few years. The pastoral introduction to the sacramentary is the *General Instruction of the Roman Missal.*

General Instruction of the Roman Missal. This document first appeared in 1969 with the as yet incomplete sacramentary. When the final version of the sacramentary appeared the next year, Pope Paul VI had added an introduction to the original General Instruction. According to Archbishop Annibale Bugnini, CM, former secretary of the Congregation for Divine Worship, the pope was intent on answering critics who claimed the reformed liturgy was not orthodox or legitimate. Nonetheless, the added introduction is helpful in giving a clear vision of the historical development of the reform.

The General Instruction is what the title says: general. As such, there is more information in it than any one minister needs for any one liturgy. It can be difficult to find the parts of the document that will answer a specific question. Adding slightly to the confusion is the fact that the U.S. version has an "Appendix to the *General Instruction* for the Dioceses of the United States." The most useful thing to do is to read through the entire document at least once, marking the sections that might be helpful later. Then, in the future, use a resource that has indexed the key words of the document. (See *The Liturgy Documents* later in this bibliography.)

Lectionary for Mass. New York: Catholic Book Publishing Co., 1970; various other publishers. The lectionary has been revised with new translations of the New American Bible and the New Revised Standard Version approved by the U.S. bishops. The NRSV was also approved by Rome, but the bishops delayed printing lectionaries with that translation until the NAB had also been approved. During the delay, Rome rescinded its approval of the NRSV lectionary and denied approval for the revised NAB lectionary. No reasons were made public, but it is often said the inclusive language used in the translations was unacceptable to the Vatican. U.S. bishops and biblical scholars (as well as Canadian bishops who had already printed thousands of NRSV lectionaries) are discussing the possible options with the Vatican as this book goes to press. The outcome is uncertain. Currently, there are three approved translations of the U.S. lectionary: the unrevised NAB (which is used in almost all U.S. parishes), the Revised Standard Version (which is the predecessor to the NRSV), and the Jerusalem Bible. The pastoral introduction to the Lectionary is the *Lectionary for Mass, Introduction.*

Lectionary for Mass, Introduction. 1970, 1981. This is a very helpful document for understanding the structure of the lectionary and the way in which readings were selected for the three cycles of the liturgical year. In addition, there are several pastoral suggestions for adapting the Liturgy of the Word that often go unimplemented because planners do not know of them. This is an especially helpful document for all the parish lectors to read—including those who proclaim the Gospel.

General Norms for the Liturgical Year and the Calendar. 1969. The Roman Calendar and the *General Norms* which govern it appear in the front of the sacramentary. Since the reform of the sacramentary was dependent on the shape of the liturgical year, the study group in charge of the revision of the calendar was among the first groups formed. The calendar was slightly revised when it appeared in the full version of the 1970 sacramentary and it continues to be revised as new saints are added to the cycle of celebration. The *General Norms* make instructive reading for all those charged with liturgical planning. Particularly helpful is the emphasis the document puts on the primacy of Sunday in the liturgical year.

Directory for Masses with Children. 1973. The DMC (it also appears at the front of the sacramentary) should be read along with the *General Instruction on the Roman Missal* not only to learn how to adapt liturgy for young people; it is also a helpful lens for understanding liturgical principles in general. The DMC is intended for grade-school-age children. If you ever wondered where children's Liturgy of the Word comes from, this is the document to read. If a parish is serious about implementing liturgy adapted for children, planners will also need to be familiar with the three eucharistic prayers for children (also in the sacramentary) and the recently published *Lectionary for Masses with Children.*

Lectionary for Masses with Children. San Jose: Resource Publications, Inc., 1993; various other publishers. This lectionary was instigated by the Federation of Diocesan Liturgical Commissions more than a decade ago. They asked the U.S. bishops to produce a lectionary more easily apprehended by young children. At least a few other versions of children's lectionaries are in use in the United States, but this is the only one approved for use in Roman Catholic worship.

Music in Catholic Worship. Washington, DC: United States Catholic Conference, 1972.

Liturgical Music Today. Washington, DC: United Staes Catholic Conference, 1982. Together, these documents comprise the standards and guidelines for liturgical music in U.S. parishes. MCW is the stronger and clearer of the two. Besides giving clear and concise principles for the selection and evaluation of liturgical music, the document provides a fine theology of celebration that is worthy of being studied even by those who are not musicians. LMT was written to fill in some of the gaps left by MCW, particularly the use of music in liturgies other than the Eucharist and the use of high technology instruments in liturgical music. In 1993 many of the principle committee members who wrote these documents along with a score of other liturgical music experts published a statement titled *The Milwaukee Symposia for Church Composers—A Ten-Year Report.* The document, although it has no official status, was intended to be a response to or updating of current thinking about liturgical music in the U.S. church for the nineties. As a document, its influence does not seem to be as widespread as MCW or LMT. However, the principles it espouses are mostly condensations of the articles, talks, and workshops that most national experts in liturgical music are putting forth today. In that sense, the things the document has to say is having an impact on the U.S. church. It was first published in *Pastoral Music* and has been reprinted by Liturgy Training Publications.

Environment and Art in Catholic Worship. Washington, DC: United States Catholic Conference, 1978. Like MCW, this document provides an excellent theology of celebration that ought to be studied by all those concerned with good liturgy. It provides a clear understanding of the nature of symbol in the liturgy and helps discern the quality and appropriateness of liturgical artifacts. EACW was written as a companion to *Music in Catholic Worship.* When read together, these documents give a developed understanding of how the full, conscious, and active participation called for by Vatican II can be practically implemented in U.S. parishes. EACW may be the best of the liturgical documents to start with for educating yourself or a liturgy committee because of its clear writing style and sound theology.

Fulfilled in Your Hearing —The Homily in the Sunday Assembly. Washington, DC: United States Catholic Conference, 1982. This is one of the most important and, sadly, one of the most under-used of the liturgical documents. The document grew out of the concern of the U.S. bishops with the quality of preaching in parishes. William Skudlarek, OSB—one of the nation's premier experts on preaching—was the principle author. Drawing on the same theological premises found in *Music in Catholic Worship* and *Environment and Art in Catholic Worship,* FIYH begins with the assembly as its starting point. "We believe it is appropriate, indeed essential, to begin this treatment of the Sunday homily with the assembly rather than with the preacher or the homily." The final section of the document is titled "Homiletic Method," which lays out a plan for not only preparing the weekly homily but also involving the parish community in the process. Even those who are not preachers should be familiar with this document.

The Liturgy Documents: A Parish Resource. 3rd ed. Chicago: Liturgy Training Publications, 1991. Most of the above documents plus a couple of others are compiled in this book, which includes helpful overviews of each of the documents included.

Rite of Christian Initiation of Adults, 1988; *Rite of Baptism for Children,* 1970; *Rite of Marriage,* 1970; *Order of Christian Funerals,* 1989; *Rite of Penance,* 1975; *Pastoral Care of the Sick—Rites of Anointing and Viaticum,* 1983; *Book of Blessings,* 1989. All of these are published by Catholic Book Publishing Co., and some are published by various other publishers. Liturgical Press, under its Pueblo label, sells a collection of these and other rituals in a two-volume set titled *The Rites.* Volume 1 includes the RCIA; Baptism of Children; Confirmation; Penance; Holy Communion and Worship of the Eucharist outside Mass; Marriage; Pastoral Care of the Sick: Rites of Anointing and Viaticum; and the Order of Christian Funerals.

Volume 2 contains Ordination of Deacons, Priest, and Bishops; Rite of Commissioning Special Ministers of Holy Communion (also found in the *Book of Blessings*); Dedication of a Church and Altar; and several other rites of less importance to the parish minister. Those involved in the particular sacraments named here should be familiar with both the ritual texts and their introductions. All parish ministers should be familiar with the RCIA and the *Book of Blessings*. Also note that the *Rite of Marriage* has been revised and was issued in its Latin typical edition in 1990. The English translation and adaption is currently in progress.

Other Books for the Liturgical Library

Adam, Adolf. *The Liturgical Year: Its History and Its Meaning After the Reform of the Liturgy.* Collegeville, Minnesota: The Liturgical Press/Pueblo, 1981.

Brown, Kathy, and Frank C. Sokol, eds. *Issues in the Christian Initiation of Children: Catechesis and Liturgy.* Chicago: Liturgy Training Publications, 1989,

Brown, Raymond. *An Adult Christ at Christmas — Essays on the Three Christmas Stories.* Collegeville, Minnesota: The Liturgical Press, 1980.

Chupungco, Anscar. *Cultural Adaptation of the Liturgy.* New York: Paulist Press, 1982.

———. *Liturgies of the Future.* New York: Paulist Press, 1989.

Congregation for Divine Worship. "Circular Letter Concerning the Preparation and Celebration of the Easter Feasts." Washington, DC: United States Catholic Conference, 1988.

Dallen, James. *The Reconciling Community: The Rite of Penance.* Collegeville, Minnesota: The Liturgical Press/Pueblo, 1985.

Davis, J. G. *The New Westminster Dictionary of Liturgy and Worship.* Philadelphia: The Westminster Press, 1986. Although written for the Anglican tradition, this is a good all-around reference book to have on your shelf.

Duggan, Robert D., and Maureen A. Kelly. *The Christian Initiation of Children: Hope for the Future.* New York: Paulist, 1991.

Dunning, James B. *Echoing God's Word: Formation for Catechists and Homilists in a Catechumenal Church.* Arlington, Virginia: North American Forum on the Catechumenate, 1993.

Empereur, James L. *Prophetic Anointing: God's Call to the Sick, the Elderly, and the Dying.* Collegeville, Minnesota: The Liturgical Press/Michael Glazier, Inc., 1982.

Federation of Diocesan Liturgical Commissions. *The Mystery of Faith: A Study of the Structural Elements of the Order of Mass.* Washington, DC: FDLC, 1981.

Favazza, Joseph A. *The Order of Penitents: Historical Roots and Pastoral Future.* Collegeville, Minnesota: The Liturgical Press, 1988.

Fink, Peter E., ed. *The New Dictionary of Sacramental Worship.* Collegeville, Minnesota: The Liturgical Press, 1990.

Foley, Nadine, ed. *Preaching and the Non-Ordained.* Collegeville, Minnesota: The Liturgical Press, 1983.

Fuller, Reginald. *Preaching the Lectionary.* Collegeville, Minnesota: The Liturgical Press, 1984.

Guentert, Kenneth. *The Young Server's Book of the Mass.* San Jose, Resource Publications, Inc., 1986. Written as a how-to book for altar servers (boys or girls), this book provides a useful outline of the meaning and history of the Mass.

Guentert, Kenneth, and Nick Wagner, eds. *The Usher's Book of the Mass.* San Jose: Resource Publications, Inc., 1996. I had heard many parishes were giving *The Young Server's Book of the Mass* to their ushers to help them better understand the flow of the liturgy, so I edited it to orient the language toward their ministry. Either book is useful as a primer for beginning members of the liturgy committee.

Gusmer, Charles W. *And You Visited Me: Sacramental Ministry to the Sick and the Dying.* Collegeville, Minnesota: The Liturgical Press/Pueblo, 1984.

Guzie, Tad W. *Jesus and the Eucharist.* New York: Paulist Press, 1974.

Hovda, Robert. *Dry Bones.* Silver Spring, Maryland: The Liturgical Conference, 1973. An excellent book on presiding from one of the masters.

Huck, Gabe. *The Communion Rite at Sunday Mass.* Chicago: Liturgy Training Publications, 1989. If every parish followed the clear, sound advice in this book, the liturgical renewal would be greatly expedited.

———. *Leaders's Manual: A Guide to Preparing Liturgy with Children.* Chicago: Liturgy Training Publications, 1988. Although originally written as a guide to using LTP's *Hymnal for Catholic Students*, this book has become the best resource available for understanding and planning children's liturgies. No parish or school should be without it.

———. *Liturgy with Style and Grace.* Rev. ed. Chicago: Liturgy Training Publications, 1984.

Huels, John M. *Disputed Questions in the Liturgy Today.* Chicago: Liturgy Training Publications, 1988. An excellent study of the liturgical and canon law dealing with lay preaching, Mass intentions, concerts in churches and more.

Jeffery, Peter. *A New Commandment: Toward a Renewed Rite for the Washing of Feet*. Collegeville, Minnesota: The Liturgical Press, 1992. This book will provide you with all the information you need to justify including women in the footwashing ceremony.

Jorgensen, Susan S. *Eucharist! An Eight-Session Ritual-Catechesis Experience for Adults*. San Jose: Resource Publications, Inc., 1994. This is the book to get for everyone who did not participate in the catechumenate process. Many parishes wish they had something like the catechumenate for the "regular" Catholics. *Eucharist!* provides a process that takes participants step-by-step through the Mass and helps them reflect on their experience.

———. *Rekindling the Passion: Liturgical Renewal in Your Community*. San Jose: Resource Publications, Inc., 1993. This book could be called the "theory" behind *Eucharist!* Using the social sciences and blending them with current theology, the author gives readers a clear insight about what is needed for parish renewal. James Moroney, chairperson of the Federation of Diocesan Liturgical Commissions said, "This seminal work opens the door for us on the true meaning of liturgical renewal."

Johnson, Lawrence J. *The Word and Eucharist Handbook*. San Jose: Resource Publications, 1993. Originally written in 1986 and slightly revised a few years ago, this is one of the best resources available for pastoral liturgy. The author provides a basic, matter-of-fact guide to each section of the Mass.

Kavanagh, Aidan. *Confirmation: Origins and Reform*. New York: The Liturgical Press/Pueblo, 1988.

———. *Elements of Rite: A Handbook of Liturgical Style*. Collegeville, Minnesota: The Liturgical Press/Pueblo, 1982.

———. *On Liturgical Theology*. Collegeville, Minnesota: The Liturgical Press/Pueblo, 1984.

———. *The Shape of Baptism: The Rite of Christian Initiation*. Collegeville, Minnesota: The Liturgical Press/Pueblo, 1978.

Keifer, Ralph A. *To Give Thanks and Praise: General Instruction on the Roman Missal with Commentary for Musicians and Priests*. Laurel, Maryland: The Pastoral Press, 1980.

Kennedy, Robert J., ed. *Reconciliation: The Continuing Agenda*. Collegeville, Minnesota: The Liturgical Press, 1987. A collection of papers presented at the 1986 summer conference sponsored by the Notre Dame Center for Pastoral Liturgy.

Klauser, Theodor. *A Short History of the Western Liturgy: An Account and Some Reflections*. 2nd ed. Oxford: University Press, 1981.

Lang, Jovian P., OFM. *Dictionary of the Liturgy.* New York: Catholic Book Publishing Co., 1989.

Lewinski, Ron. *Guide for Sponsors.* 3rd ed. Chicago: Liturgy Training Publications, 1994.

Loret, Pierre. *The Story of the Mass: From the Last Supper to the Present Day.* Liguori, Missouri: Liguori Publications, 1982.

Mitchell, Nathan, and John Leonard. *The Postures of the Assembly during the Eucharistic Prayer.* Chicago: Liturgy Training Publications, 1994.

Morris, Thomas H. *The RCIA: Transforming the Church.* New York: Paulist Press, 1989.

Nelson, Gertrude Mueller. *To Dance with God: Family Ritual and Community Celebration.* New York: Paulist Press, 1986.

Patterson, Keith L. *Evaluating Your Liturgical Music Ministry.* San Jose: Resource Publications, Inc., 1993. The title is self-explanatory, and there is no other resource like this available. The author outlines a step-by-step process for evaluation and improvement of a community's liturgical music that not only involves the music ministers but the entire parish.

Powell, Karen Hinman. *How to Form a Catechumenate Team.* Chicago: Liturgy Training Publications, 1986.

Power, David N. *Gifts That Differ: Lay Ministries Established and Unestablished.* Collegeville, Minnesota: The Liturgical Press/Pueblo, 1980.

———. *Unsearchable Riches: The Symbolic Nature of Liturgy.* Collegeville, Minnesota: The Liturgical Press/Pueblo, 1984.

Rutherford, Richard. *The Death of a Christian: The Order of Christian Funerals.* Rev. ed. Collegeville, Minnesota: The Liturgical Press/Pueblo, 1990. Originally written for the Rite of Funerals, this book was revised after the new rite was published. It is the most comprehensive work available on the history and theology of Catholic funerals.

McBrien, Philip. *How to Teach with the Lectionary.* WHERE: Twenty-Third Publications, 1992.

Searle, Mark. *Christening: The Making of Christians.* Collegeville, Minnesota: The Liturgical Press, 1980.

———. *Liturgy and Social Justice.* Collegeville, Minnesota: The Liturgical Press, 1980.

———. *Liturgy Made Simple.* Collegeville, Minnesota: The Liturgical Press, 1981.

Searle, mark, and Kenneth Stevenson. *Documents of the Marriage Liturgy.* Collegeville, Minnesota: The Liturgical Press/Pueblo, 1992.

Stevenson, Kenneth. *To Join Together: The Rite of Marriage.* Collegeville, Minnesota: The Liturgical Press/Pueblo, 1987.

Talley, Thomas J. *The Origins of the Liturgical Year.* Collegeville, Minnesota: The Liturgical Press, 1986.

Wilde, James A., ed., *When Should We Confirm: The Order of Christian Initiation.* Chicago: Liturgy Training Publications, 1989.

Yarnold, Edward. *The Awe-Inspiring Rites of Initiation: The Origins of the RCIA.* 2nd ed. Collegeville, Minnesota: The Liturgical Press, 1993.

Periodicals

Many journals, magazines, and newsletters focus exclusively on liturgy or touch on liturgy as well as a number of other subjects. Many of them are fine publications. By grounding yourself in the primary liturgical documents and by examining the articles found in the publications listed below, you will be able to judge for yourself what other periodicals you wish to subscribe to.

Modern Liturgy. Resource Publications, Inc. 10 issues per year. I am obviously biased, but I have to recommend that you subscribe to this magazine. It is edited for the same person this book was written for. That is to say, ML is intended to be read by the average person in the parish who is concerned about good liturgy. It is not necessarily for someone who has studied liturgy in school. The only liturgical training someone needs in order to be able to understand the articles and advice in ML is to be a regular participant in the liturgy. ML focuses on the sensual, artistic quality of the liturgy as well as the practical "how to" of making Sunday worship better in your parish.

Catechumenate. Liturgy Training Publications. 6 issues per year. This journal is especially for those involved in initiation ministries. It ought to be read even by those only involved in infant baptism preparation or the confirmation process. The articles often focus only on the rites of the catechumenate but in doing so give a good overall theology of initiation.

Assembly. Notre Dame Center for Pastoral Liturgy. 5 issues per year. This periodical is not very long—usually about eight pages (8.5" x 11"). However, it is one of the best things available for giving an overview of particular aspects of the liturgy or the liturgical year.

GIA Quarterly. GIA Publications. 4 issues per year. This is well edited and thought provoking.

Church. National Pastoral Life Center. 4 issues per year. *Church* tries have a broader focus than just liturgical issues, but much of its material seems to focus on the liturgy and the liturgical renewal. It is a fine journal and offers an interesting mix of editorial content.

Pastoral Music. National Association of Pastoral Musicians. 6 issues per year. Each issue contains scholarly and pastoral writing on topics specifically for the parish musician.

Bishops' Committee on the Liturgy Newsletter. United States Catholic Conference. 10 issues per year. This newsletter (usually eight pages) can sometimes be a little dry, but it is the "horse's mouth" for getting the official scoop on the latest liturgical developments.

Index

Books for Your Liturgical Ministry

(Bulk Prices Available)

THE USHER'S BOOK OF THE MASS

Editors of MODERN LITURGY

Paper, 80 pages, 4" x 7", ISBN 0-89390-364-7

Help your ushers understand the basics of the Mass—and why their role is so important. This book tells ushers about the structure of the Mass, the symbols used, and how their ministry contributes to the flow and prayerfulness of the Mass.

LITURGICAL MINISTRY: A Practical Guide to Spirituality

Donna Cole

Paper, 64 pages, 5½" x 8½", ISBN 0-89390-372-8

Working under the assumption that all liturgical ministry is important and should be prepared for prayerfully, Donna Cole uses the commissioning rite as the basis for the liturgical minister's formation.

THE YOUNG SERVER'S BOOK OF THE MASS

Kenneth Guentert

Paper, 72 pages, 4" x 6", ISBN 0-89390-078-8

Here is the history of the Mass in the language of young people. With this background, servers can understand why they do what they do. You'll be pleased with the results: your servers will feel and act like a special part of the liturgy.

LECTOR BECOMES PROCLAIMER

Jerry DuCharme & Gail DuCharme

Workbook Edition, Paper, 80 Pages, 8½" x 11", ISBN 0-89390-158-X
Original Text Edition, Paper, 80 pages, 4" x 6", ISBN 0-89390-059-1

Help lectors understand the difference between proclaiming and reading the Scripture lections with these helpful preparation techniques and delivery tips. The workbook edition shows you how to implement a series of training workshops.

Call 1-800-736-7600 for current prices. See last page for order information.

Resources for Making Your Liturgy Even Better

THE WORD AND EUCHARIST HANDBOOK — REVISED EDITION
Lawrence J. Johnson

Paper, 168 pages, 6" x 9", ISBN 0-89390-276-4

The Word and Eucharist Handbook is your complete reference guide to liturgy. Designed for worship planners, ministers, and liturgical artists, it answers your questions about the origin, development, and modern practice of each part of the Mass.

CATECHISM OF THE CATHOLIC CHURCH ON LITURGY AND SACRAMENTS
Jan Michael Joncas

Paper, 64 pages, 5½" x 8½", ISBN 0-89390-348-5

A thought-provoking analysis by a noted scholar and workshop presenter.

EUCHARIST! An Eight-Session Ritual-Catechesis Experience for Adults
Susan S. Jorgensen

Paper, 200 pages, 8½" x 11", ISBN 0-89390-293-4

> "Respectful of differences, open to the variety of approaches, ready-to-use and well designed, *Eucharist!* is a strong resource and strong spark to our ritual imagination." — *Catholic Press Association Book Award Judges*

REKINDLING THE PASSION: Liturgical Renewal in Your Community
Susan S. Jorgensen

Paper, 272 pages, 5½" x 8½", ISBN 0-89390-236-5

> "This seminal work opens the door for us on the true meaning of liturgical renewal." — Rev. James P. Moroney, Chair, FDLC

Order from your local bookseller, or call toll-free 1-800-736-7600, fax 1-408-287-8748, or write to:

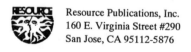

Resource Publications, Inc.
160 E. Virginia Street #290
San Jose, CA 95112-5876